GARY ROBERTSON, born and bred in Dundee, of the city's culture and dialect. His three also performed, have sold out all 47 shows. 2 reality TV show *SAS: Are You Tough Enough?* Having performed hundreds of poetry gigs, he was awarded Performer o' the Year at the inaugural Scots Language Awards in 2019. As a musician, he is the lead singer, lyricist and bagpiper for local band The Cundeez, who have played both nationally and internationally. He is also a self-confessed fitness fanatic, martial artist and mountaineer and completed all of Scotland's Munros many years ago. Aside from all this, he enjoys his day job as a Council binman, but his great love above all else is spending time with his wife, Sue and his family.

By the same author:

Gangs of Dundee (Luath Press, 2007)
Pure Dundee (Luath Press, 2007)
Skeem Life: Growing Up in the Seventies (Black and White Publishing, 2010)

Wild Mountain Times

GARY ROBERTSON

Luath Press Limited
EDINBURGH
www.luath.co.uk

First published 2025

ISBN: 978-1-80425-237-6

The author's right to be identified as author of this book under the Copyright, Designs and Patents Act 1988 has been asserted.

The paper used in this book is recyclable. It is made from low-chlorine pulps produced in a low-energy, low-emission manner from renewable forests.

Printed and bound by
Robertson Printers, Forfar

Typeset in 11.5 point Sabon by
Main Point Books, Edinburgh

Illustrations by Les Cameron
Photographs by Gary Robertson and members of
Dundee NCR Hillwalking and Climbing Club.

© Gary Robertson

Contents

	Preface	9
	Introduction	11
	Acknowledgements	13
The Bothy Culture		15
1	From Factory to Mountain and Glen	17
2	Fae the Horse's Mooth	24
Corrour Bothy		34
3	The Road an' the Miles	35
4	Glencoe	43
The Bothy Fire		55
5	Carry On Camping (Part 1)	57
The Sourlies Moose		71
6	The Yellow Submarine	73
7	The Ghillies	78
Peg Leg Meets The Plegosaurus		86
8	The Dangerous Brothers	90
9	Carry On Camping (Part 2)	97
10	Skye's The Limit	110
Hale Bop an' a Fosbury Flop		131
11	Is There Anybody There?	135
12	Hold The Line	146
A' Chùil, A' Chùil, We Ah Fell Doon		159
13	Big Flatters	162
14	The Highland Hullabaloo	168
15	The Quick Way Down	174
16	The Bothy Culture	186
	Epilogue	197

For those whom we have shared summits, glens, blizzards, bars, tents and bothy fires with, and to those whom we have yet to meet.

Preface

I BEGAN EMPLOYMENT with the NCR company in 1990, and it was there on the factory noticeboards where I first became aware of the Hillwalking and Climbing Club and stared in wonderment at the places which they were visiting all over Scotland on both Day and Weekend Meets. It's fair to say it was one of the greatest decisions I ever made in my life to join the club.

It truly was the best group of people I could ever have hoped to meet, many of whom are still some of my best and closest friends today. Having purchased some very basic gear and worn jeans, cotton t-shirts, woolly jumpers and totally 'not waterproof' waterproofs on the early meets, I realised I had found my happy place and quickly fell in love with a pursuit that was to become a huge part of my life. The monthly adventures with like-minded characters fuelled my body and mind like an insatiable drug. A massive part of my own fulfilment was testing my fitness levels and pushing the barriers of challenge far beyond most things I had done before. With a healthy group of members already involved in completing the Munros, it was a natural progression to follow suit.

In doing so, it grew to be something much bigger and profound than just bagging mountains on a list. Essentially, it was the key to opening the door to Mother Nature herself and embracing the simple things in life. The unrivalled scenery, the wildlife, the weather, the hardships, the beauty and camaraderie were all free for those who dared to walk the walk.

And then there was the chaos and hilarity, for what is life without being exposed to danger and a bloody good laugh along the way? The characters involved throughout the long history of the club were (and are) from a mostly working-class background, and this was (and is) reflected in the genuine attitude, resilience and hardiness whilst 'oot on the hill'. The at times hard drinking 'aff the hill' latterly became part and parcel of the highly anticipated meets. This in turn created stories, whether under canvas, in bars or in bothies or totally hungover on a mountain of which you are about to read.

I began this writing venture and chronicled history of the collected tales of our club around 15 years ago, during which other projects got in the way and inevitably delayed the process. I most gratefully gained a further 15 years of mountainous mayhem to add to the story.

Some names have been changed to protect the guilty, the innocent and also those who wear buffs or use walking poles, take no drink or coal into bothies, can't use a map or compass, don't say 'hello' to strangers on a hill, call out the Mountain Rescue when they have diarrhoea, nausea or anxiety, don't know the words to 'Dark Lochnagar', turn up in the bar still wearing a climbing harness and loads o' jangly things, call a loch a 'lock' and a glen a 'valley', wear a t-shirt proclaiming 'I've done the West Highland Way' or 'NC 500', or those who ask on social media, 'I'm doing a Munro, what's the weather like on Tuesday in Torridon?'

The outdoor stage has had many NCR performers down through the years, and I was extremely privileged to play a small part in the hugely colourful production of our 'Wild Mountain Times'.

Introduction

IT'S FAIR TO say it has been a wee while since Dave Brown and Ian R Mitchell's timeless classic book *Mountain Days & Bothy Nights* landed in our hands to entertain us with hilarious memories of bygone days and nights spent in the Scottish mountains, glens, bothies, howffs, dosses, caves and other creative dens in which to get one's head down for a night or two. Their tales of life in the mountains and the wonderfully colourful characters who were in their company and whom they also encountered while having a wee dram or two round a glowing fire have become the stuff of legend for all who have had the pleasure of reading it.

The time seemed right then to finally put pen to paper and write *Wild Mountain Times,* and in doing so, bring to life the history of the Dundee NCR Hillwalking and Climbing Club and the men and women who were there and still go out to this day. The title is, of course, a play on words from that beautiful Scottish folk song *Wild Mountain Thyme*, but on the pages which follow, you will definitely struggle to find any mention of the famous herb. You will, however, read of times which were indeed wild and sometimes chaotic, where more often than not the demon drink was involved. The great love, first and foremost, was always the mountains, the unmatched beauty of the Scottish landscape, the rich and incredible history of our land and its people and the unquenchable appetite for challenge and adventure in getting away from the humdrum life in the city. With a largely working-class membership coming from the NCR factory itself, the pull of the pub and the urge to 'hae a wee swally' was never far away, which in turn led to episodes of high jinks, capers and riotous behaviour at times, although in fairness, this progressed as the years went by and wasn't the case in the beginning. It was interesting to read in the aforementioned book above, the quote from the writers along the lines that 'ya just dinna see the big numbers or groups goin' oot any mair'. It's just a pity that our paths never crossed at some point, as the NCR club was most certainly 'oot' and indulging in the banter and craic, whether it was rough camping or gathered around a roaring fire in some remote bothy.

The stories within, however, are not solely focused on the wild times. During the club's long existence, there have sadly been accidents with a few resulting in death and the very real nature of mountaineering and the dangers it can bring become all too apparent. We hope that in writing this history, we can honour all of those who have gone before us and remember with love and affection the great memories they have left us with.

The interviews conducted with some of the founding members were thankfully located, and along with original pieces written for the *NCR Magazine*, this provided the most important part of the jigsaw – the beginning. Sadly, a few of these characters have passed to the great bothy in the sky, and again, it is with huge thanks to these pioneers that the story can begin. We hope you will enjoy the journey around Scotland and some of its islands as we take you camping, sleeping in 'coo' sheds, marching into bothies in the middle of nowhere, the summits, the unspoilt glens, the blizzards, the gales, the midgies, the clegs, and the mad characters who held up the bars. Oh, and we've chucked in some bothy poetry for good measure, so go and pour yirsels a large one, put a spark to the fire and kick aff yir clumpy baits, sit back, chill oot and let us shoulder the packs as we tak ya through oor crazy journey.

Acknowledgements

FIRST AND FOREMOST, I would like to thank my wife, Sue and all my family for always being there for me and believing in all the various paths my journey takes. Each and every one of you make it a joy to wake up each morning and keep me going.

To my close friends, and, indeed, any of you whom I can proudly call friends, I give my sincere thanks for the comradeship, laughs, tears and every other aspect of life that fills the gaps in between.

To my fellow mountaineers, you all know who you are. Thanks is not nearly a big enough word to describe how grateful I am for the wonderful mental times we have all shared. Here's to many, many more.

My deep and enduring gratitude goes to Frank Anderson and all the early members who started this brilliant club way back, and those who followed to provide the foundations on which to build a most colourful and eventful story. Their pioneering ventures into the mountain landscape and the enthusiasm they took with them shall never be forgotten.

I can't thank the NCR Company enough, firstly, for setting up in Dundee and giving so many people some much-needed employment and secondly, for supporting a hillwalking and mountaineering club. The factory magazine was an invaluable source of rich material from the very early meets and I am wholly indebted to all contributors who shared their little stories, and, of course, to everyone who shared their wonderful photos.

A barrel of thanks to my good friend Les Cameron, who did all the amazing illustrations.

My final acknowledgement and huge thanks go to Gavin MacDougall and all the incredible staff at Luath Press, Edinburgh, who once again have turned my words into a book which I hope will be enjoyed for many years to come. Your unwavering support is very much appreciated.

Coire Fionnaraich bothy

The Bothy Culture

A place but no' jist any place
A place in the middle o' sumwahr
A place wahr legwork is a must
A place withoot yir car
A place tae laive the Rat Race
An' share a fire wi' friends
A place tae pass a bottle roond
An' sample malts an' blends
A place tae meet the Devil
The Devil in us a'
An' dance a reel wi' demons
While angel pipers bla'

A place fir summer solitude
Or a winter mountain base
Visions o' a cosy flame
While on an ice-clad face
A place tae rid the world o wrangs
An' debate the best o' rights
A place wahr room has turned tae ring
An' seen some bloody fights
Aye, a place that welcomes characters
Bringin' life tae four stone walls
That's the 'Bothy Culture'
I'll go… when her voice calls

Dedicated to the late, great musician Martyn Bennett, who coined the phrase 'Bothy Culture' for his second album.

CHAPTER 1

From Factory to Mountain and Glen

A place that welcomes characters

IT WAS 11 June 1947, and the day dawned fair at Camperdown as the city of Dundee prepared to welcome none other than the charismatic figure of Colonel Deeds, the NCR Chairman from America. Along with other company representatives and civic dignitaries, they were gathered to witness the opening of the company's first manufacturing plant in Britain.

Dundee had beaten off some stiff competition nationwide to secure a working partnership with our American cousins, which would last right through to the beginning of the next millennium and beyond. With the Second World War still very much fresh in the memory, there was a huge need to rebuild the country and get it moving again. The coming of the NCR (or National Cash Registers to give it its proper title) provided massive employment opportunities, which would only grow from strength to strength in the following years. Eager workers queued up to be part of this new workforce assembling these cash registers with the promise of good conditions and attractive wages.

The US ideology of providing excellent welfare for its employees certainly carried over the Pond, and it's fair to say anyone working for NCR was seen as part of an extended family. Facilities such as medical care and catering of a very high standard were other welcome additions for the blossoming factory community. As the early success of the company grew, so too did the chance to enjoy recreational activities, and a whole explosion of clubs and organisations sprang up as a result, undoubtedly helped by workers having a little extra in their pockets to spend.

Employees were able to choose from a vast array of activities, sports and pastimes such as golf, table tennis, basketball, whist drives, cricket and rock n' roll dances, among many others. For those adept in the art of playing music, specifically the bagpipes, there was also the opportunity to join the pipe band, and for the budding actors and actresses among the workforce, there was the Amateur Operatic Society, who would put on performances on local stages and, on some occasions, even in the factory! And of course, not forgetting the football team (the 'Cash' as they and the Organisation were nicknamed) who would go on to win the Scottish Amateur Cup in 1965.

And so, to our story. The NCR Hillwalking and Climbing Club was formed in 1949 by Frank Anderson. Frank had been a keen walker and climber before the War, and it seemed a natural course to form a club for those like-minded souls who wanted to get away and explore the great outdoors. Other characters such as Gibby Gray, Tommy Thompson, Dorothy Paladini, H. Coutts, K. Fairweather, W. B. Thompson, Roland Jackson and Jim Heaney were among those who formed the nucleus and founded the club. Another Dundee club which had formed slightly earlier was the Càrn Dearg, and it wasn't uncommon for people to have a dual membership and, in doing so, get out on alternate meets.

The very first day meets were to the Angus glens of Clova, Glen Doll, and Lochnagar, a little to the north of the aforementioned. These were the much-loved areas where the club would return to regularly (and still does to the present day). According to the early memories of Frank and Gibby, when interviewed, a real motley crew turned up wearing all sorts of gear and most definitely not equipped for the mountain environment. The outcome was predictable, as a few were never seen again. On the subject of gear, for those hardy souls who stuck it out, it was a case of beg, steal, borrow and acquire by any means necessary. Unlike the modern-day mountain-goer, where hundreds and in some cases thousands of pounds can be spent on kit. But this was post-war, and ex-army issue was abundant and was gladly accepted by many of the budding and enthusiastic hillwalkers and mountaineers. Old raincoats and capes provided some protection for the upper body while commando rucksacks and other assorted packs carried the pieceys. Kapoc quilts issued to the ATS (Army Territorial Service) were fashioned into sleeping bags, and if you could procure a pair of sturdy army boots, then you were well on your way. For those able to obtain the 'Tricouni boots' or, to be precise, boots with Tricouni nails in them, this was the popular footwear of the day, which would serve a walker or climber well and gave good grip, certainly on rock. The highly acclaimed Vibram rubber soles, which became universally popular, were not affordable till much later for many. For winter, the ice-axes were, of course, the heavy wooden shafted variety and a sure way to build up some arm strength.

Frank's sister Betty remembered a neighbour who used to work on the whale fishing boats and managed to supply some top-quality kit from Norway, much to the envy of fellow members. In sharp contrast to 'appropriate' outdoor gear, it was rather comical to come across an early Club photo from the 1950s in Glen Clova, where a few of the men were decked out in three-piece suits complete with shirt and tie and some of the women were resplendent in their 'Sunday best' fashion wear.

One amusing memory Gibby shared was on a day meet to the Lomond Hills in Fife and walking with a character from the club known simply as 'Aald Wullie', who he recalled was in his mid-70s. As they walked uphill and chatted, Gibby suddenly noticed the conversation halting and the pace gathering momentum. He whispered to himself, 'that aald bugger's wanting to beat me to the summit!' The younger man did arrive first, but not a big enough gap for Aald Wullie not to see him bent over and devouring some much-needed oxygen.

The older athlete proclaimed, 'yir breathin oot yir erse there son!' Gibby could only laugh and agree with the competitive old-timer.

From the days of the club's birth, some of the original members had sought more than a plain old day meet and had ventured out for an overnighter or a weekender, often accompanying the Càrn Dearg club on one of their organised meets. It wasn't until the latter end of the 1950s that any proper organised NCR weekend meets began, and the club was able to travel further afield, opening up a whole new adventure with camping and the occasional bothy trip and Youth Hostel. Tents were picked up, borrowed and bought and mostly made of heavy-duty canvas, which weighed a ton, especially when wet, and so discouraged heaving them into anywhere more than 20 ft from the road. As long as it was a roof over the head and stood up in a storm, then the occupants were as happy as Larry. For cooking and haein' a wee biley-up, Primus stoves were used, burning paraffin or meths, but campers had to be extremely careful when putting a match to the fuel they had pumped up. Too much pumping and giving it laldy with the little knob could result in a roaring fireball with a loss of eyebrows and hair at best, or a worst-case scenario of tent inferno and a real battle for survival. (We will warm to this latter subject shortly – pun intended.)

Public transport was utilised and folk would hop on the bus from Dundee to Perth, then board the Milk Train to walk the Lairig Ghru through the Cairngorms. Gibby would sometimes travel north on an old Royal Enfield motorbike and meet up with others who had made the journey for the designated meet. On one such visit to Glencoe, Gibby and his pal Jim Carson had chosen a route to climb in the 'Lost Valley'.

(On a purely personal note, I've never for the life of me come to terms with using the word 'valley' in Scotland, especially in such a historical glen as this).

With surroundings almost prehistoric in nature and expecting the odd brontosaurus to amble through, whilst maybe catching a glimpse of a soaring pterodactyl, onwards and upwards they progressed, spurred on by the fact that there was no record of this climb ever having been done. Excitement was building to fever pitch as they took it in turn to lead and began exchanging possible titles for this new climb.

'How aboot J and G's?' gasped Jim, pouring out his creative juices to the max.

'Or G and J's?' returned Gibby, equally as creative and delving deep into the realms of originality, all the while both of them laughing as they went higher. All mirth, merriment and expectations died, however, as they pulled themselves onto a ledge and found a discarded, empty sardine can. They sat there for a moment, utterly dejected while viewing their prehistoric panorama then burst into uproarious laughter. Such is life. In all honesty, there was probably a more likely chance of meeting a dinosaur than a fellow walker or climber in those days, as folk recalled that one could walk for days and never see a soul.

Glen Clova and Glen Doll have always held a special place in the hearts of Dundonians, being the nearest of the big mountains and what we would regard as the beginning of the Highlands from our side. The same can be said for towns such as Forfar, Brechin and Kirriemuir and it was to Kirrie that members would get the bus from the old station in Dundee's Lindsay Street and deposit into the local Cosy Corner pub for a few foaming ales, awaiting the arrival of Jim Fern and his bus. By all accounts, Jim was a bit of a character, and he would run the group up as far as the Clova Hotel. On approach, he would shout 'tickets an' tanners please' which was the cue to dig deep into your pocket and provide a wee 'backhander' to continue the extra three or four miles to the road's end at Glen Doll. Later, he would return and take the happy hikers back to Kirrie. (It is sad to think that these times have long passed into hazy memories, and along with it, the wonderful Jim Fern's of this world)

The burgeoning club brought opportunities to travel beyond the city boundaries, which for many a factory worker would have seemed unimaginable in years gone by, given the fact that most could not afford a car or even the fare for transport. The sense of adventure was strong and every journey, whether it was near or far, was embraced wholeheartedly. The NCR business was growing rapidly, and with that success, there came an even stronger bond between owners and employees. Wages and conditions increased, and a Sports and Social fund was set aside to help all the clubs and organisations within. The Hillwalking and Climbing Club were given a loan of a minibus which could carry up to 12 bodies. Frank and Gibby were sure this was an old hearse which had been converted, but any ghoulish thoughts of what had previously occupied the vehicle were quickly snuffed out when it was stated that the fuel was all paid for and the driver came free. Now, being from working-class backgrounds and not ones for missing a trick, the driver pulled Gibby over on return from one of those first meets and whispered, 'Ya ken, that bus has stull got plenty fuel in it?'

'Aye an' what o' it?' replied Gibby, wondering what the statement implied.

'Well, ehl come up the morn's night, syphon it oot an' git yir motorbike filled up.' And with a wee tap of the index finger on the nose, a lift of the eyebrows and a nod of the head, the gentleman's agreement was sealed.

It seems quite alien, and some may say laughable, in this modern era of being able to drink late into the night in pubs and clubs, when not so long ago it was shutters down at 9.30pm. An early story recalled the time when the club were up enjoying a few well-earned drinks in a local hostelry in Braemar following a cracking day on various mountain tops. As the time approached 9.30pm, in swaggered the well-known local bobby PC Florence, who was a native of the Western Isles. He was out of uniform and in civvies and obviously looking for an after-hours dram or two himself, so he told the men politely but firmly to 'drink up and get out.'

One of the lads boldly stood up and questioned the Hebridean in-comer. 'Wut do ya mean? Yir no' even in uniform!'

The retort was fired back in a decisive but warm island lilt, 'Yesss, but if I wasss standing here naked, I could still arrest yisss all, now get out gentlemen and oidhche mhath!'

There was never really a drinking culture as such during those early years, and women rarely attended the weekenders, but gradually that began to change. There was, however, the beginning of the bothy culture and visits began to shelters, such as Ben Alder Cottage (McCook's), Blackburn of Pattack and a bothy which was a favourite with the Aberdeen lads situated at the far end of Loch Muick called, rather predictably, Loch End bothy, which is sadly no longer. Youth Hostels were also used on occasion.

And so it was, with Frank Anderson, Gibby Gray and friends' original enthusiasm, vision and comradeship, the NCR club was established and well on its way to exploring much of what this wild, rugged and beautiful land had to offer for walkers, climbers, campers, dossers and adventurers alike.

CHAPTER 2

Fae the Horse's Mooth

Corrour bothy

THE FOLLOWING SELECTION of excerpts (of which there were many) was passed on by ex-employee Brian Mann, who uncovered these 'gems' in old copies he had of the *NCR Magazine,* which was written and printed in-house for well over 60 years. They provide excellent first-hand accounts of the very early meets dating from the Spring of 1949 through to the 1960s and indeed complement the interviews held with Frank and Gibby. They have been kindly reproduced in their original dialogue.

It was very interesting to read just how far and wide the club were venturing back then, from Glen Clova to Ben Lawers, Aviemore, Braemar and the Cairngorms, Glencoe, Ben Alder and the Isle of Skye, to name a few. However, these all seem like a walk in the park compared to Bill Wilson's epic hitchhike to Switzerland in 1953 to climb the mighty Matterhorn. Given the road conditions in Scotland back then and the speed (or lack) of vehicles, along with a shortage of funds for use of public transport, the logistics of getting to Skye must have seemed like a visit to the edge of the world. Switzerland must have felt as far off as the moon!

We can appreciate all the more what these people achieved, given their fairly primitive gear. In addition to this, there certainly wouldn't have been the vast access to information regarding routes, climbs, etc. So, it is all the more inspiring to learn that some were climbing to a very good standard and also utilised these skills to form a small and active Rescue Team. Others were competent skiers, which would have required a determined effort, given the fact that there were no tows to assist, whilst many (as was evident from photos) were truly content to just live a moment in time in the Scottish landscape.

May 1949
Rambling

A group of members of the Rambling Section took full advantage of the April holiday by going for a weekend's hill-climbing in the Glen Clova area. The route taken from Clova Hostel was by Braedownie and then, after a steep ascent, they reached the Capel Mounth. Here, the going became difficult due to rather deep snow.

The path then led to the east head of Loch Muick and by a rough road, the remaining nine miles to Ballater were accomplished, passing Linn o' Muick on the way. The return journey was made via Glen Muick and the base of Lochnagar. The intention was to climb Broad Cairn, but due to misty weather, this was abandoned. Before the party set off for home, they walked up to view Loch Brandy, then dashed down quickly to catch the last bus!

June 1949
Rambling

It's said that a human being requires eight hours' sleep to maintain a normal, healthy condition. This fact was completely overlooked by ten members of the Rambling Section who, on Saturday, June 11, decided to join the climb up Lochnagar, which was being organised by Davie Glen, a local man with 20 years' experience of mountaineering.

We met in a quarry at Braedownie where we were joined by Willie

Mitchell and Andy Wood, together with one automobile, four dozen 'smokies' (smoked haddock) and two dozen eggs from Arbroath. After a hearty high tea, we set off on the first stage of our journey following the course of the South Esk river before climbing steadily up the Capel Mounth. At 11.30pm we started the ascent proper, and by this time, there was a fairly large party. After a final brew-up and meal (our last before breakfast next morning), we tackled the steepest and roughest part of the climb, where we were joined by the main party. We were told by a gillie that a climber had been seriously injured the previous afternoon after a fall of 120 ft.

We reached the highest summit of Cac Càrn Beag in the wee small hours, and there, assembled all around, were nearly 150 bodies hailing from many parts of Scotland, including our organiser and well-known mountaineer Davie Glen, complete with eagle feathers in his bonnet. At 3.50am the sun appeared amid cheers from the onlookers, and as it got brighter, the rays coloured the mountain mists a soft rose pink. We departed the peak in a biting crosswind and reached Loch Muick at 7.00am, where we had breakfast before heading back over to Braedownie and the waiting buses to take a very sleepy crowd home.

July 1950
Snowdrifts Trouble Ramblers

A party of NCR hill climbers left Dundee at 10.35pm on Friday, 19 May, bound for Aviemore, where they intended to start walking to Blair Atholl via the Lairig Ghru Pass and Gleann Teilt. Aviemore was reached at 4.30am on Saturday morning and the party immediately set off to traverse the Lairig, a very old right-of-way through the heart of the Cairngorms. The Boulderfield was crossed without any real mishaps, although rocks hidden in snowdrifts proved rather troublesome. The descent was made in good time and dinner in Corrour bothy was ravenously devoured.

After dinner, there were several anxious moments when members of the party had to ford the River Dee to get back on track, all the while watched by the huge sentinel of The Devil's Point. Rain then began to pour down, and the mountain tops became shrouded in mist as the going got a bit tiresome. The party intended to stay the night in Bynack Lodge, and this was reached at approximately 7.30pm on Saturday.

A roaring fire was built in the old kitchen of the lodge, and a very merry evening was spent swapping yarns and having a sing-song to scare away ghosts which may be about, as the place is said to be haunted.

An early start was made on Sunday morning and the nice weather made the walk through Gleann Teilt very pleasant. Blair Atholl was reached at around 5.30pm after a distance covered of roughly 40 miles, then shortly afterwards, we boarded the bus for home.

K. Fairweather

November 1950
Mountain-Top Rescue

On the weekend of 2/3 September, three members of the NCR Hill Climbing Section accompanied the Càrn Dearg Mountaineering Club on one of their monthly outings. A party of 34 persons left Forfar bound for Glencoe and arrived there at about 8.00pm on Saturday after a five hour bus journey. Some of the Càrn Dearg members camped near the base of the Buachaille Etive Mòr, which they intended to climb the next day. The rest travelled on, some camping at the foot of Clachaig Gully while the others stayed the night in the Youth Hostel.

The next day, led by Davie Glen, a party of 12 set off to traverse the Aonach Eagach ridge beginning on Sgòrr nam Fiannaidh and heading east, where they were rewarded with some magnificent views including the Mamore Range, Nevis, Loch Leven and Bidean nam Bian. The descent brought them out at the meeting of the Three Waters around 5.00pm on Sunday, and following a hearty meal, they began packing to head home. At 6.30pm a lone climber came off the Buachaille Etive Mòr with the news that two of the Càrn Dearg had become cragfast (stuck) on the last pitch of the Raven's Gully (a very severe climb near the summit).

A rescue party immediately set off and climbed to the top of Raven's Gully via the Great Gully and Cuneiform Buttress. After a great show of teamwork, the two trapped climbers were hauled out by ropes, none the worse for their ordeal. The descent in the rain, mist and pitch darkness took seven and a half hours, and rescuers and rescued finally arrived back at camp around 5.00am Monday, all feeling very tired and wet. The bus arrived back in Forfar at 11.00am, where the company dispersed, bringing to an end a rather hectic weekend in Glencoe. *K. Fairweather*

(The downplaying and almost innocent writing of the above account masks the complete seriousness and danger in which the two climbers found themselves stuck high on the rock and without the luxury of modern communication, must surely have worried for their lives during this frightening ordeal. Without the slightest peep of negativity (and having just scaled the Aonach Eagach), these superhuman characters showed incredible stamina and endurance to then race up the Buachaille and successfully carry out a rescue mission for their stricken friends, not to mention what was surely a horrendous descent. Then back to the bus and on their merry way. Real and genuine men o' the mountains – they don't make many like that these days!)

June 1952
Compilation of Meets

Sharp, cold and snowy conditions greeted the quartet of Frank Anderson, A. G. Gray, J. Carson and J. R. Jackson early on the morning of 1 January as they boarded a train to Blair Atholl, where they walked 11 miles to Tigh na Cruaiche bothy at the foot of Beinn a' Ghlò.

Searching for wood for the fire was no light job and the party had to range as far as a mile and a half before they had collected sufficient fuel for their needs. Although they all felt quite cosy, when they awoke next morning, they found their boots and socks frozen stiff. As Glen Tarff is new territory to the members of our Section, they spent much time exploring, and it was moonlight before they returned to the bothy. The next morning, they made their way back down the Glen accompanied by a local shepherd and his flock.

Jan/Feb 1952

January and February have been fairly quiet months in the activities of the NCR Hill Climbing Section, as the roads in the glens have been so blocked with snow that it has been virtually impossible to reach any of our favourite spots. This does not mean, however, that members have been idle and some gully climbing was had in Corrie Fee, one of the finest corries in the Grampian Range.

Another recent meet was held to Ben Lawers on the north shores of Loch Tay, Perthshire, where half of the party climbed to the summit, surmounting many difficulties in the icy conditions, while the other half enjoyed themselves skiing on the lower slopes not far from the hotel.

April/May 1952

Club members spent the Spring holiday in Glen Nevis climbing the 'Ben' and were delighted when the weather cleared to reveal an astonishing mountain panorama, which proved the icing on the cake for a thoroughly enjoyable trip.

The following weekend, 28 employees and their friends travelled to Glen Clova, where they broke into two parties, one tackling Jock's Road while the other went over the hills to Loch Muick and back via the same route.

Still going strong, we spent the next weekend at Ben Alder on the shores of Loch Eireachd. There, again, we were fortunate to enjoy some lovely views of the surrounding peaks, some of which were still plastered with snow.

To round off a busy few months, we paid a visit to the 'Lost Valley' in Glencoe. This is really a 'corrie' high above the floor of the glen. The rocks are honeycombed with caves, but members took the more civilised course of pitching their tents. The weather on this occasion was not too kind for us, but the trip was most enjoyable, nonetheless.

A. G. Gray & F. Anderson

August 1953
Conquest of Wellenkuppe

'Steamed-up goggles, frozen ropes, crevasses, crumbling footholds and powdered snow were some of the hazards encountered by Bill Wilson (Machine Shop) and his little party when they went to the Swiss Alps.

During the summer holidays, the author and a small party of climbers set off with high hopes of climbing the Matterhorn in Switzerland. Before leaving Dundee, they made the usual preparation for passports, vaccination certificates and traveller's cheques, but, as they intended to hitch-hike, little time was spent on travel arrangements.

On the first evening, they got as far as Doncaster. The next night, they camped at Seven Oaks and, by Sunday night, they had reached Calais. None of the party had any real knowledge of the French language, so it took a little time and patience on both sides before they could indicate their requirements for shops and hotels, but the use of sign language ensured they made their way steadily south via Paris. Late on Wednesday night, they reached Berne in Switzerland. It looked like a very simple matter to cross over to Zermatt, but due to the difficult terrain, they had to detour down to Montreux, then back up the Rhone Valley. From Visp, they had to take a train up the steep cogwheel track to Zermatt, which lay at a height of 5,310 metres above sea level.

Booking in at a hotel, they then began to look for a guide to take them up the Matterhorn, but the information that the fee would cost something in the region of £20 soon put an end to this hope! Not to be downhearted, they decided on an alternative plan and, with careful study of their maps, they agreed that the summit of Wellenkuppe would be their objective. The fact they had no guide did not distract them as they had gleaned valuable information from local people who were always willing to help in any way they could, and so, with borrowed ice-picks, they set off in gloriously warm sunshine for the 12,500 foot peak. They resisted the temptation to indulge in frequent rests and steadily made their way up the zig-zag path to Rothorne Hut at 10,000 ft. Inside the hut, they prepared a meal and were in bed early.

The next morning dawned dull and heavy, very uninviting for climbing mountains. However, after travelling hundreds of miles to get there, they did not feel like admitting defeat now. The first obstacle on the way up was the Trief Glacier. This was no easy task, especially when one peered into the deep crevasses which stretched menacingly on either side of the line of climbers. They had to traverse a wide, snow-covered area until they eventually reached the base of a steep rock face.

The usual minor discomforts had to be faced. Goggles steamed up, ropes froze, hands felt twice their normal size, and breathing was difficult, but at no time did anyone feel like giving up. Scaling the rock face was a hazardous journey as foot and handholds loosened at the slightest touch, and the least sound of falling rocks from above froze the party dead in their tracks. They were to find the descent even more perilous as powdered snow filled in their tracks almost as soon as they were made.

Although they were disappointed at not managing to climb the Matterhorn, the conquest of Wellenkuppe, especially in view of the conditions during the latter part of the climb, was ample compensation.

February 1955
Skiing and Climbing

The weather has not been congenial to all of the outdoor Sections, but the hill-climbing enthusiasts have welcomed the hard conditions. On the New Year weekend, they headed for Inverness-shire and camped near Glenmore Lodge in the Rothiemurchus Forest – glorious country and quite good conditions for camping.

There was not much snow for skiing, but the party passed the time pleasantly walking and climbing on An Càrn Gorm.

Since then, they have had two short trips in Angus, to Glen Clova and Glen Prosen in arctic cold, but Frank Anderson (Toolroom) says conditions were splendid with plenty of skiing in soft snow.

September 1959
Weekend Meet to Lochnagar

The Hill-Climbing Section held a very successful meet to Lochnagar on September 19/20. This is only the second time we have organised an official, complete weekend outing, and it was very well supported. The party travelled by bus to Loch Muick, where the majority camped and the remainder spent the night in Loch End bothy, just across from Glas-allt-Shiel. This bothy is an old shooting hut built on the shores of Loch Muick. A very enjoyable evening was spent in the bothy, where a few candles and a huge log fire served to provide the only lighting for the proceedings.

Three of the party travelled over the hills from Glen Doll, arriving at the bothy around 2.00am and were so quiet they did not wake the rest. Conditions next day were not too good as it was very misty and windy on top of Lochnagar; however, everyone had an enjoyable day and the bus going home that evening, though filled with tired bodies, was also filled with lusty singing.

Dorothy M. Nicholson

These then were just a small selection from the many pieces written by former club members and provided a nostalgic wee look back to days much changed from the present. Sifting through them, it was amazing to read that as far back as 1955, there were 40 employees and friends attending some of the day meets. Journey times of three hours to get to Glen Clova from Dundee and Forfar and five hours to Glencoe are an indication of just how different and time-consuming travel was.

A little story worth relating was a day meet in October 1958, where 30 members went to climb the Munros of Dreish and Mayar in the Glen Doll area. Before they even began the ascent, they had to cross the River Doll by means of a makeshift, dilapidated old bridge. Both peaks were gained in thick mist before a steep and difficult descent in pouring rain via Corrie Fee (which most certainly wouldn't have had the well-worn path that many enjoy nowadays). For one member of the party, however, this must have been nothing short of a nightmare as he carried his baby daughter all the way in a framed padded seat strapped to his back. They made bairns tough back then!

One humorous episode was told by Frank Anderson as some members tried to locate the peaks of Lochnagar while battling over the boulder-strewn summit plateau in misty, windswept conditions. Also in the vicinity were members of the Torry Club from Aberdeen. As one of the NCR party, (who was a very well-known, prominent and somewhat zealous breed of firebrand Shop Steward) staggered around while being buffeted from the wind, a lone figure lurched out of the grey mist and in a strong Aberdonian accent asked, 'Are you a member o' the Tory party?'

Witness accounts diplomatically told of the fiery Union man's reply being 'lost' in a conveniently passing violent gust of wind. The poor Aberdonian native must have been truly flummoxed as to what he had said to send the NCR man into such a rage.

The final little piece worthy of any note was to learn that in the Spring of 1960, the club had purchased its very first tent for use by members who didn't have or couldn't afford one. It must have been a fair size as the writer said it could accommodate 'quite a few bodies'. This then was the real beginning of something which the club was able to build on in later years, with the help of a fantastic yearly funding package from the NCR company. Many members who were to pass through would benefit from the fine selection of Vango tents and, also, crampons and ice-axes.

Corrour

Born in 1877, grown fae a seed o' stone
You've worn a guise o' Hell an' Heaven, a loner all alone
A speck on the Lairig Ghru, the highway through a Cairngorm heart
An artery giein access to, glens an' mountains on an ordnance chart

In summer the River Dee weaves ballads, while stealin' by yir door
But sweet melody becomes invalid, when winter unleashes the lion's roar
An' the Devil stands content, guardin' the climber's lair
While Macdui an' Carn a' Mhàim repent, fir the company ye keep sae sair

A candle in yir windee draws, a lost soul in the night
Gled tae shelter within yir walls, an' shake the hand o' kind respite
Aye many have used yir refuge, or 'fridge' as yir sometimes known
But beggars an' choosers show gratitude, when the teeth o' a blizzard are shown

Yiv played host tae Osama Bin Laden, or so it wiz scribed on the wall
Wi' Bush an' Blair baith maddened, Al Jazeera had a broadcast ball
The Dalai Lama also says 'he wiz there', wut a perty ya must've had
While ane wiz spoutin' death an' fear, the ither smoked pipes o peace in yir pad

'Lonely, bleak, freezin' Corrour', the jury returned 'not guilty!'
Bothy life's wut ya mak it fir sure, a haven fir thanks an' humility

CHAPTER 3

The Road an' the Miles

Ben Alder bothy

BEFORE WE GET on the road and travel the miles through this chapter, I feel it is pertinent to mention a character of some stature and note who worked for the NCR throughout the 1950s, '60s and into the '70s. Indeed, to call the man Syd Scroggie a 'legend' would be wholly justified. Syd was first and foremost a 'man o' the mountains' and well known throughout the Dundee climbing fraternity and far, far beyond. Much has been written and documented, and justifiably so, about his incredible life story as well as appearances on TV, most notably as the guest of Eamonn Andrews on *This Is Your Life* in 1964 and a guest spot on an episode on Weir's Way with the delightful and equally legendary character, Tom Weir.

An accomplished mountaineer, skier, writer, poet, scholar, soldier and so much more, Syd was an inspiration to all the lives he touched and never let his debilitating war wounds resulting in him becoming blind, and the loss of a leg hold him back from living a truly remarkable life. Many of us who joined the club in later years never knew him personally or were ever out on the hill with him, but it is with immense pride that we regard him as 'ane o' oor ane fowk'. Frank Anderson and others took Syd out on occasion, accompanying him locally and further afield and on one visit to Ben Alder bothy, Frank laughed loudly as he recalled arriving late at night with bodies strewn all over the floor and falling over poor Syd, who was tucked up cosy and sleeping soundly in his bag. The fact that Syd even made it into the bothy shows the fierce willpower and tenacity of the man, as anyone who has made the long arduous march (from any direction) will agree, the terrain can be extremely tough and challenging at the best of times.

His connection with the NCR club remains warm in our hearts. Fitting it is then that the cairn erected in his honour on Balluderon Hill in his beloved Sidlaws (or 'Seedlees' as they are affectionately known in Dundee) stands proudly viewing the mountains to the north whilst allowing him uninterrupted views south over his adopted city.

As the years and the decades rolled by, the club had stabilised and indeed grown in popularity and numbers had swelled with day meets and weekend meets regularly very well attended, so much so that by the early 1970s the decision was made to hire a bigger bus. Previously, all sorts of transport had been used for the weekenders, and even an old ambulance had seen some alternative service (which reportedly broke down during a meet to Deeside and remained there for years, occupied by local chickens).

Davidson's, a bus company from Forfar it was who provided a 52-seater coach and a driver for the weekend and so began in earnest the era of fully enjoying the drink, the craic and the walking and climbing. With women and couples also in attendance on many meets, it made for a proper party atmosphere and the long journeys north and west were embraced by all. There was hearty sing-songs, and the need to have a wee Corries' number or two tucked up the sleeve was a bonus when called upon to 'dae a wee turn'. The obligatory pub stop on the way broke up the journey, but the intended half-hour stop more often than not rolled into an hour and a half or more and getting the revellers out became a nightmare. Things became even more boisterous when characters such as the Gibb brothers, Arthur and Derek, would turn up with a fiddle and guitar as well as others like Jock Tosh and Colin Westwood, who were famed for singing about the ss Shieldhall, the Glasgow 'shitey' ship which transported the city's sewage. The mobile party on board would then depart into the pub and take over (in a nice way), which surely would have had the publican rubbing their hands with this unexpected jovial rabble's arrival.

Bruce was ten years old in 1974 when he was taken on his first weekender with his dad Alex, who worked alongside Frank Anderson in the factory. He had already been walking regularly in the Sidlaws and had done a bit of climbing with his father. The destination was Kintail, away in the far north-west of the country and an area of mountainous majesty where rugged peaks fill the skyline in almost every direction. It was to be a baptism of fire for the young lad, or rather, horizontal driving rain and a thunderous gale while marching over the towering Five Sisters. Many youngsters would have told their dads where to go after a serious undertaking such as this, being utterly soaked to the bone, but Bruce was already showing he had the necessary attributes to grit his teeth and battle on for one so young. His next meet upped the ante considerably as the club camped in Glen Nevis and Bruce was taken over one of the classic climbs on Ben Nevis – the daunting and commanding Tower Ridge. Frank knew all the routes and saw a real talent in the keen and enthusiastic young lad. Bruce remembered being around three-quarters of the way up the route when 'this man' appeared from nowhere, having seemingly climbed straight up the side. This man was none other than club member Davie San, who had been eagerly necking pints and drams for fun in numerous hostelries in Fort William the night before and, by all accounts, was totally steaming. He had never been on Tower Ridge in his life and had decided to join them after a hangover-dispersing tent fry-up and a cup of tea. As one of the emerging regulars from that era, Davie was to prove a real powerhouse on the hills and equally so in the raucous pub sessions, which became more frequent with a growing element of the weekenders.

With colourful characters aplenty among the older heads, the young Bruce couldn't wait for the Friday night walk with his dad from the St Mary's housing scheme down to the Dunsinane factory, fully laden with all their gear to see what adventure and location lay ahead. Wullie Batchelor was a joiner in the factory and would cut a pile of wood and fill an old oil drum to be used as a brazier for the campsite fires. The chosen sites were always for rough camping. Official campsites were never used as that would mean spending valuable drink tokens on two nights' fees, which was out of the question. This infuriated the owner of the site at Shiel Bridge near the aforementioned Kintail in particular, as these tent 'villages' would appear very late on a Friday night, straight across from the official site and with it, a big loss of potential revenue. In the mornings, Frank would be round checking on everyone before they hit the mountains and top people's tea up with a tot of whisky, even Bruce's.

'Here ya go son, this'll pit hairs on yir chest.'

At 13 years old he thought this was brilliant and considered himself well and truly on the way to becoming a real man. During these early teen years, he was taken on his first serious rock climb on Coire Etchachan in the Cairngorms – a crazy climb he remembered – that was him hooked. Some of the lads from Forfar, which lies only 13 miles to the north of Dundee, began to get involved and a good climbing relationship was forged with a healthy, friendly rivalry.

Around the winter of 1977, when Britain was in the tight grip of 'Anarchy In The UK' and the sneering, spitting, rebellious tones of Punk Rock, Bruce and his dad, along with the rest of the club, had opted for the less riotous pastime of camping near the shores of Loch Laggan in the central Highlands. The duo had the mighty Creag Mèagaidh firmly in their sights and set off into the imposing Coire Àrdair with the weather growing ever more wild and fierce around them. The snow conditions were rock hard as they neared the summit plateau, and the wind had kicked up into a major hoolie. The decision to abort was a sensible one, and they began the fairly steep retreat, descending down Easy Gully.

After a short while of careful down climbing, Bruce unfortunately misplaced his crampon onto the other, lost his balance and very quickly took off on an uncontrollable slide. There was no chance of stopping with a self-arrest as the ice-axe was flailing about, frequently smashing into his face. The situation was critical, and there was absolutely nothing his father could do but watch and pray and hope with all his heart that his son came to a safe halt. Somehow, after a very swift and terrifying drop of several hundred feet and with the loop of the axe amazingly still around his wrist, it miraculously stuck into softer snow and with a violent and abrupt yank, he stopped. The pain in his wrist was instant and excruciating. Alex descended as fast and safely as he could to see if his son was still alive. Thankfully, he was, but blood was pouring from facial wounds where the ice-axe had struck, which seriously worried his father. Bruce was more concerned with his wrist, which was dislocated. With some twisting, pulling and screaming, they managed to pop it back in, relieving some of the intense pain. In shock and clearly shaken, they both walked out of the gully and into the little hut, which used to be situated at the bottom of Raeburn's Gully and thanked their lucky stars a hundred times over.

As they headed back to the tent with Bruce licking his wounds, his father stopped and said 'Son, not a fuckin' mention to yir mither aboot wut jist happened here or wull no' git back oot ever again!'

'Dinna worry dad, eh slipped on an icy path. Remember?'

'That's ma boy.'

They both let out a nervous laugh, knowing full well they had got away with a massive escape from serious injury, or worse.

As Bruce matured, so too did his fitness and competence as a climber and he and his father became a formidable team, taking on some big days in the mountains, such as tackling The Saddle in the morning, then over the Five Sisters in the afternoon, while on a trip to Kintail. One Friday, as the bus weaved its way through Glencoe, the duo jumped off and headed into the Lost Valley to pitch their tent. Both were up early with the lark and flew over Bidean nam Bian and down to the Clachaig Inn where the question was raised, 'do we hit the bar fir a couple o' pints?' The tempting thought was quickly banished, and they were soon standing on the summit of

Sgòrr nam Fiannaidh at the western end of the Aonach Eagach where they met the bus driver who asked if they'd take him along the ridge. No sooner were the words out and they were heading east, swarming over each airy pinnacle, all the while guiding and reassuring their raw recruit. Safely down on terra firma and with a thanks and cheerio, the driver took the long walk back to the bus and a no doubt well-earned forty winks while the two trojans sought the sanctuary of their tent high in the prehistoric-like setting of the Lost Valley, guarded by a magnificent mountain fortress.

Geordie F (who in later years was to become Club president and at the time of writing, still holds that position) remembered the tales of adventure and excitement his secretary would bring into the NCR office on a Monday morning following a weekend away with the club in the late 1970s. He agreed to give this 'hillwalking malarkey' a try and went out with his son on a day meet to Ben Vorlich in the Perthshire Highlands. The budding mountaineers turned up wearing wellies and jeans and carried their pieceys in an old haversack and enjoyed it so much that Geordie put his name down for the forthcoming weekender to Kintail, which had become a firm favourite for many, so much so that he recalled there being around 90 folk in attendance travelling up on two 52-seaters. The locals must have thought a new township had sprung up on the Saturday morning as a vast array of tents covered a wide area, all rough camping, of course. Geordie had managed to borrow a tent from his brother-in-law, but the word 'tent' was a very loose description of what was actually in the bag. It contained two poles, a ridge pole, a piece of canvas and no pegs, so rocks were sought and gathered to ensure some kind of shelter was erected. Without a carry mat and only a battered old sleeping bag to kip in, the spartan conditions were made decidedly more uncomfortable as squadrons of the infamous west coast midge descended wave after wave to attack at will. (This latter scenario was indeed a complete shock to the system for any east coaster or southerner on their first visit into midge enemy territory). All the hardship, pain and discomfort of that debut weekend were soon forgotten, however, as Geordie was rewarded with some of the finest views in Scotland while climbing over the Five Sisters in glorious weather.

Some of those early bus journeys encountered the inevitable mishap, and during yet another trip to Kintail, the bus trundled to a weary halt at Ballinluig, Perthshire, on the A9 and refused to go any further. An emergency phone call was made back to the depot in Forfar, where the strict order came back to 'stay with the bus, we'll get another one out as soon as we can.' The stranded mountaineers' response was predictably rebellious, 'Eh that'll be bliddee right! Ok, abdee inta the Ballinluig Hotel fir a light refreshment!' On entry, the dulcet tones of a Country singer could be heard crooning his way through some classic song of how the cowboy's lover had left him to run off with another and now, huddled around the embers of a dying fire with his faithful horse, he delved into his cold beans and reflected on where it had all gone wrong. At length, the back-up bus did turn up, but no one can remember how they got to Kintail or how the tents got up.

For some, it must have seemed like the A9 held a curse on the bus at times as somewhere near Dalwhinnie it spluttered, coughed, then came to a standstill on a bitingly cold and clear October evening. Amid the groans and moans, two worthies at the back of the bus were heard above most of the others.

'Ach fir cryin' oot loud, wut the hell's up wi' this heap o' shite now?'

'Eh dinna ken Tam, but ehl awa doon the front an hae a word wi' the driver, see wut the crack is.'

The driver, who was the son of the owner, was already out, head in the engine assessing and re-assessing and with much scratching of the head and thoughtful rubbing of the chin, he proclaimed to the disgruntled worthy and the others, 'We seem to hae fuel starvation folks. I'll get a phone box and call back to base, see if they'll send another bus oot.' With no boozer within marching distance, the agitated group just had to sit tight and wait for the cavalry to arrive, which it duly did, albeit much, much later. On boarding the crippled bus, the more experienced driver was able to locate the problem in no time at all, then flew into what was described as 'a bit of a rage' while confronting his fellow employee.

'Fuel starvation, eh? Fuel fuckin' starvation? There's NAE bloody fuel in it! You've let it run dry, ya clown!'

No one who was there can remember (either deliberately or by choice) what the verdict was from the jury of that swiftly assembled roadside kangaroo court.

The following little episode was not of the 'mechanical' breakdown variety but more of the breakdown in 'human willpower' to reach the planned meet out west at Cruachan in Argyll. The windscreen wipers on the bus were working flat out to maintain any kind of visibility as torrential rain and a howling gale lashed violently on a hellish night. On the A85 road to Crianlarich, the Luib Hotel was fast approaching, and someone made the call to 'pull in for a couple of pints' in the desperate hope that the storm might pass. With a warm welcome inside, a band rattling through a set of rocking stompers and the flow of quality ale, the decision was made to stay put and camp around the back of the pub. As appealing as this new development was, not all members were in agreement, and the threat of civil war within the ranks was very apparent as rebels argued the fact that no one had brought maps for that particular area and that they should stick to the original meet no matter what.

The moral of this little tale went along the lines that they all had 'the best weekend ever' and the rebels who had voiced such vociferous opposition to the altered plan the previous night, were found to be the first patrons at the bar Saturday night with their arses planted firmly on the accompanying stools and doing their very best to wade through the fine selection of ales and malts.

CHAPTER 4

Glencoe

A roaring bothy fire

FOR THE NCR club, the dawning of the 1980s began where the previous decade had left. In terms of membership and numbers in attendance on both day and weekend meets, the club was as strong as ever. Things would gradually change, however, as the decade progressed, with weekend meets being particularly affected. This was due in part to the bus company, which had been a stalwart servant to the club over the years, eventually going bust. Numbers sadly dropped from the heady days of 50 on the bus down to 30, then latterly down to a dozen or so as the unreliability of whether climbers would actually get to the mountains and, more importantly, back, became a real worrying issue.

The day meets largely remained unaffected, as other buses were used, but slowly, as with any club, the clientele changed as new members came and older ones went. The era of 'Munro bagging' wasn't really a thing with members during this time, but certainly by the end of the '80s, a new breed appeared on the scene and set about the list with a passion.

For now, we head west again to what was (and still is) a real favourite on the calendar, no matter what time of year – Glencoe. The glen itself, once the ancestral home to a branch of the Clan Donald, is steeped in raiding parties, clan warfare, lawlessness and of course, the scene of one of Scotland's most dark and treacherous acts by the government of the day on February 13 1692, forever known as 'The Massacre of Glencoe'. For those who have read the history, it is very hard not to think of those bloody events from that period of turmoil and picture the scene in one's mind whilst driving or walking through that deep cut and almost intimidating glen where giants rise menacing and foreboding on either side.

The club nearly always chose the western end to camp, which was conveniently situated right outside that most ancient and famous of mountaineering bars, the legendary Clachaig Inn. These, of course, were the days when it was still acceptable to rough camp in that vicinity, much to the annoyance of a certain nearby official campsite who must have counted the number of tents assembled each weekend and, with it, lost revenue. Down through those years, claims and allegations were made by some enraged campers that dark forces were at work where, on return from a day on the hill, their tents and possessions would be found uprooted and lying in a ditch.

For many good years, the location provided the ideal spot for mountaineers, biker rallies and generally, those who just wished to party like crazy in what many regard as one of the best pubs on the planet. One of the problems, which was blatantly obvious and possibly proved the eventual downfall of being allowed to camp there, was the lack of toilet facilities. This was National Trust for Scotland land and a real magnet for tourists. The last thing a bus full of excited sightseers wanted to see, having spent the last three days comfortably travelling on their luxurious coach to Scotland from Hampshire or the like and marvelling at the stupendous views, was a big hairy biker's arse dropping a log in the heather.

On a glorious May morning in 1982, while the dew sparkled from the first light of sunrise, a team of younger members arose from their slumber and decided over breakfast that today was the day that Clachaig Gully would be conquered. The first ascent by W. H. Murray in 1938 and epically described in his classic book *Mountaineering in Scotland* would inspire generations of climbers for years to come. And so, it was a mixed team, some with rock climbing experience, some just brave and daft enough to get involved, which set off for one of the most visible and ominous features in the glen with high hopes, trepidation and a few butterflies to accompany the freshly downed breakfast. One who fell into the 'brave and daft' category in the nicest terms, of course, was Jonesy. Initially, the boys were progressing well and dealing competently with all obstacles presented. Higher and higher they went. Jonesy was enjoying the experience and impressing his fellow climbers as he took each pitch in his stride. He felt this was his time and insisted he would lead the next pitch, so, rather reluctantly, the boys agreed. Anyone who knows Scottish gullies understands it is not normal rock climbing at times, and more like waterfall climbing on slimy, wet rock. Jonesy had only gone about 20 ft up with poor protection when he slipped off. The protection came out, and down he crashed, landing on his back at the feet of the anxious party. Thankfully, he had a rucksack on which took most of the shock, but he was in massive pain and their position was pretty desperate given the location.

Bruce figured he could attempt to climb out via the left-hand wall, as no other volunteers were stepping forward. The terrain was steep, craggy, grassy in places and very unnerving, but with extreme care, it may just be possible to scale. Just as he was getting to the top, a head popped over the edge, whooping and howling like a banshee. It was none other than Davie San, who, on completing the Aonach Eagach and now descending, had heard the commotion in the gully and saw that it was his friends in need of help. After a while of much toil and effort, they rigged up a simple pulley system and managed to haul the injured man out. Bruce and Davie, both knackered from their exertions, headed down and straight into the Clachaig for a few liquid pick-me-ups. It was some time later before the rest of the team dragged Jonesy down and straight into the bar also, where he decided his best form of defence against the pain was attack and proceeded to get steaming drunk to numb it. The nightmare ordeal continued, however, with a most uncomfortable, sleepless night in a tent before a visit to A&E on the Sunday, where it was confirmed, he'd broken the small ribs at the bottom of his back. The hapless Jonesy never pursued his fledgling climbing career again.

Above the background din of a packed Clachaig bar, ambitious plans were being hatched between two groups for an epic race over the Aonach Eagach the following day. Rated as one of the narrowest ridges on mainland Britain, with airy pinnacles and steep drops on both sides, this was to be no simple undertaking, as the mountains were completely plastered in snow with full-on winter conditions. The challenge would be a serious test of winter climbing skills, stamina and endurance. Both teams would assemble at opposite ends of the mountain and race past each other to see who got back down to the road first. (On a personal note, I have no idea how this competition was to be judged, as these were pre-mobile phone days, and the final result could be anybody's call.) As the rounds of beers poured in, claims and counterclaims were fired back and forth between the opposing members as to who would win.

The Sunday morning dawned crisp and bitingly cold, but conditions were perfect as blue skies set a postcard scene behind the jagged white peaks. Any signs of hangovers and grogginess would have to be wiped out as the battle loomed ever closer between the two parties. Bruce was in the team who were starting from the west end. With him was a guy from the former country of Yugoslavia (who was over visiting and had joined the club for the meet), along with a few of the usual suspects. Also in the group was Nick, who, with no disrespect, was considered more of a hillwalker than a winter climber, but he assured the rest he was up for the demanding task ahead.

Just as they arrived on the summit of Sgòrr nam Fiannaidh, with the whole of the ridge lying east, they noticed the bonnie blue sky had given way to a darker and brooding grey one. The wind had picked up considerably, and the signs didn't look promising, but they hastened onwards as every second counted. Both teams were going well, with the east team possibly slightly ahead when they passed, exchanging light banter as they did so in the worsening conditions. The technically challenging pinnacles were dealt with, and behind them, as they approached the final steep climb of Am Bodach. The Yugoslavian guy was in great form and stormed up it at pace. It was at this point that Nick proclaimed quite matter-of-factly to his companions, 'That's it.'

'What do you mean that's it?' asked Bruce, slightly concerned. Nick's answer turned Bruce's mood into one of grave concern, while the weather played its part and turned from awful into horrendous.

'Ehv hud enough. Time oot, meh life's ower. Jist leave is here.'

The men nearly fell off the ridge in shock at their mate's statement. The situation was now desperate. The Yugoslav guy was waved back down, and they tied the knackered Nick onto the rope, then climbed the steep face and, with a monumental effort, pulled their friend up. The race was now well and truly off as the more pressing need to get down safely took precedence. With the hours passing and darkness already upon the long overdue party, the others had struck camp and taken their friends' tents down and now waited anxiously at the Lost Valley car park, hoping they weren't going to have to contact the Rescue services. Eventually, the head torches appeared and, with much relief and cheering, they were back on the bus and Dundee bound. After the day's events and high drama, one question was left till last as the bus weaved its way along the A82.

'Wut ane o' yooz hud the 'scud books' (adult magazines) in the tent then?'

The bus went into uproar while the guilty man remained silent.

In times of peace, relations between Scotland and the 'Auld Enemy' of England have remained largely friendly for the most part with swords, battle axes and the muskets of yesteryear replaced with light-hearted banter and general piss-taking on both sides, well maybe with the exception of sporting events whether it be football, boxing or Tiddly Winks, when old rivalries can rear up once more, and for the duration of a game or a match the common theme is all-out war.

And so it was, a large English force had gathered on the banks of the Clachaig pool table (which used to be situated close to the bar and was the cause of many a near riot, when, on a packed night some reveller took umbrage to getting a misplaced pool cue poked up their arse or in the back of the head, or the player would have his match-winning shot nudged by some passing drunkard) and were holding court which upset the surrounding Scots force who were looking to get a few games themselves. The mood became tense with insults being exchanged, and the atmosphere grew thick enough to cut with a claymore.

One of the Forfar boys, fuelled up with Dutch Courage and ten pints in the system, broke rank and stepped forward with the age-old opener which ensured one almighty square-go would kick off.

'Mon then ya bastards!'

This was duly met with a whopping right-hander which nearly sent the brazen infantryman all the way back to Forfar. The battle of the Clachaig erupted like a mini-Bannockburn as combatants flew into each other with determined passion and ferocity. The heavily outnumbered NCR boys were taking a hammering as the English force drove their opponents across no-man's land and into the vicinity of the doorway. Bruce remembers being punched out through the swing doors on several occasions, only to rub his bloodied nose and get right back into the melee. He finally threw in the towel after another jaw rattler and sat licking his wounds on the grass while his brave companions made one last stand. A huge Englishman whom no one could get near had been dishing out haymakers to anyone stupid enough to get in range. Pep, using tactics which Robert the Bruce would have been proud of, waited until the hulking knockout merchant had turned blind side, then, with great guile and cunning, seized his moment and leapt onto his back, instantly grabbing hold of the man's handlebar moustache. The Englishman burst through the doors and outside, screaming holy murder as Pep pulled for all he was worth. Bruce howled with laughter as he shouted words of encouragement to his friend, 'Hing in there Pep, yir daein great!'

He did let go eventually, but didn't check to see if he had in fact 'done great' and showed a clean pair of heels to the wounded

English bear. The Scots had, like so many times in battles gone by, suffered a heavy defeat on home turf, but with Pep's suicidal actions, the battered and bruised men had found a new hero in their midst who would go down in club folklore.

An evening where the English lads may not have been so keen to get involved was during a February weekend which coincided with the nearest date to the anniversary of the 'Massacre of Glencoe'. The Clachaig was packed as usual, with the band giving it laldy in the corner when the door swung open and in marched a contingent of modern day Jacobites. These guys wouldn't have looked out of place at the time of the massacre in the late 1600s, decked out in the proper garb of the day with traditional kilts, sarks, jackets and bonnets. They were also heavily armed with traditional weapons of dirks (large daggers) and broadswords. Scotland is quite unique in the fact that anyone can dress up in traditional wear and legally walk the streets or head into a pub carrying a large knife and a broadsword, and no one really bats an eyelid.

The guys were obviously part of a society which re-enacts historical events and would be going to hold a memorial service to pay their respects at the monument in Glencoe village the following day. But first, there was some hard drinking to be had, which they indulged in full tilt. At one point, one of the Jacobites was getting into the party spirit a little too keenly and began stabbing the roof with his broadsword. Quick as a flash, the barman shouted over the noise and the music, 'Ho! I dinna mind ya enjoyin' yirsel but dinna go wreckin' the pub wi' that bloody sword!'

The Jacobite realised he'd maybe gone a wee bit too far and acknowledged with a wave and a reply of 'oh aye, sorry pal,' then continued gulping his pint. Later that night, as some of the lads were cosying into their sleeping bags, a boisterous rabble was heard staggering along the single-track road past the tents singing 'we hate the Campbells, we're gonna do them.' Joe T called over to them, 'Ho mate, thirz a Campbell in the tent next tae mine.' Thankfully, they were too drunk to respond or didn't hear, but that didn't stop poor Duncan (who wasn't a Campbell) from worrying that his expensive tent may have been shredded by some wild slashing broadswords and him being dragged away into the night to meet his bloody fate.

The Campbell Clan as a whole have been historically blamed for the massacre, and although there were a number of Campbells with the government troops who carried out the treacherous and cowardly act, the true blame lies in a much more politically complicated chain of events.

The Clachaig of old really was that kind of place with bouts of wild chaos and great craic, where sometimes, climbers would be challenging each other to see who could get the farthest round the inner walls without touching the ground, or people having a competition to header out the ceiling tiles while pogoing to 'Anarchy In The UK'. There was also a great tradition that when any of the bar staff were leaving for pastures new, at the end of their last shift behind the bar, the other staff would throw buckets of cold water (it may have been beer slops) over them as a parting gift. This would be totally unimaginable nowadays and probably result in a sacking and suing case for the perpetrators. Intrigued to see if the old plaque was still there, I recently popped into the Inn and sure enough it was still there, albeit now located inside the building, as I'm sure it used to have pride of place on the outside of Reception. I am, of course, referring to the infamous 'NO CAMPBELLS or HAWKERS' plaque, which, in these ultra politically correct days, is encouraging to see that past events are not 'brushed under the carpet'. Sure, times have changed massively, but the Clachaig is still, without doubt, one of the best climbers' bars in the country.

The glen itself is by far one of the most photogenic and popular in the whole of Scotland and provides excellent opportunities for walkers, scramblers and climbers alike to test their skills. This is most evident during the winter season when mountain craft, knowledge of conditions, competence and ability count for everything. For a group of three budding winter mountaineers, these skills counted for nothing as they set off early one December morning to climb Stob Coire nan Lochan via Broad Gully, then onto Bidean nam Bian, the highest mountain in Argyll. Ronnie Mac was the more experienced of the three with Big Betty and Wee Ecky relative novices to the winter game. It should be pointed out Betty was not of the female persuasion, but had earned the nickname from some obscure comical slur, the reason for which has been long lost through the mists of time.

Very little had been done in the way of research, certainly in terms of snow conditions for the route, and the practice of 'just going for it' was to become a common trait on many occasions for both new and experienced members alike. The trio left the A82 road and ploughed laboriously up the Coire nan Lochan pass through knee-deep snow before Ronnie remarked, 'That's oor gully there. Wull git a piecey an' a cuppa then git wired in.' Spirits were high, but not for long as they entered the gully proper and realised the enormity of the task in front of them. Progress was agonisingly slow as ridiculously deep snow, chest high in places, barred their way up. All three took turns at swimming through the white powder hell, with Wee Ecky eventually being placed at the back for fear of losing him in the depths. The fact that they were all in serious danger from an avalanche was naively swept aside as they continued to forge a deep channel upwards.

A joint decision was made to get the hell out of the gully and climb onto the ridge to the right, as the left wall looked impossible. Unbeknownst to them, this was the graded winter climb of Dorsal Arete, so called because of its shark-like fin appearance. Onwards and upwards, they waded and waded with many rock features obliterated under the deep snow. As the ridge narrowed somewhat, they came to a halt while the thickening mist and spindrift swirled wildly around. From their precarious stance, they could see a steep drop falling away to their right. Wee Ecky looked at Big Betty, and he, in turn, looked at Ronnie, then politely asked, 'Wut the hell are we on? We signed up fir a nice winter's walk in the Coe but ended up on the fuckin' Eiger!' It was at this point where, if the pair had filled their breeks in fear, no one would have judged or held it against them. In fairness, they could have climbed all day and all night and still be nowhere near the summit. It was time to get off, but how? What the small group lacked in winter experience, they made up for rather naively, in gung-ho courage and down climbed a highly dangerous section for a bit before deciding their 'easiest' option was to go back into the avalanche prone Broad Gully. In the poor visibility and engulfing whiteness, it was hard to tell how deep the drop was, so they resorted to throwing snowballs (not at each other) to see where they landed. A short descent and in they jumped with reckless abandon like three gambling desperadoes at a table involved in a deadly game of Russian Roulette.

Lady Luck was with them that day as the tons of snow, which could have devoured them in an avalanche, miraculously held firm and gave them safe passage from the gully.

The final episode in this chapter was to play out slightly to the west of the previous encounter, but with the same goal of climbing Bidean nam Bian. A group of ten members assembled outside their tents and viewed the perfect winter conditions on a bitingly cold but sunny February morning. Those who had over-indulged in the Clachaig the night before were about to board a snowy treadmill of thigh and lung burning hell on top of the standard burst heads.

From Loch Achtriochtan, they laboured steadily upwards and into the floor of the corrie. Three of the group had done some studying with aspirations to tackle the 450 metre mixed snow and ice climb of Summit Gully on Stob Coire nam Beith, one of Bidean's adjoining tops. With very limited experience of any kind on major winter mountaineering routes, this was more a case of dabbling and dipping the crampons into the realms of the Sherpa gods. There was obviously no need for ropes, harnesses, helmets, belays or ice screws because nobody had brought any on the weekend. They did, however, all possess crampons, two had an ice axe each, and Johnny 'V Diff' must have been designated leader as he had TWO axes.

The rest of the group accompanied the Edmund Hilary wannabes to the foot of the gully, where everyone stopped to observe the scene in front of them. For the intrepid three, the alarm bells should have rung, the red alert lights should have flashed, and the baseball bat with the word DANGER carved into it, smacking them in the face, should have been enough of a warning to abort, for all around lay the debris of a recent large avalanche.

With much high hopes and enthusiasm, the trio said their goodbyes and set about the task ahead. The larger group watched as they struggled upwards in the deep snow, taking one step up and, more often than not, sliding two steps down before they were finally out of sight. The magnificent seven opted for the safer but arduous slog through knee-deep snow up the corrie, passing by the sentinel top of An t-Sron on the right. As they peched and cursed their way slowly towards the ridge, a cry rang out from one of the stragglers at the back, 'Hey, look lads, it's Spiderman!'

There on the huge west face of Stob Coire nam Beith was a lone figure inching their way skywards, the only dark feature on a beautifully intimidating frozen white tapestry.

Charlie broke the silence and piped up, 'Their Spider senses must be tinglin' coz one wee slip there an' wull see a trail o' shite fleein' doon that cliff at a hunder miles an oor!' The group laughed nervously, hoping the solo climber was competent and skilled enough to complete what to them looked like a suicide mission. On reaching the lofty summit of Bidean, they were rewarded with a stunning alpine panorama with peaks caked in snow as far as the eye could see. They were also surprised to see their comrade Johnny V Diff, who was chomping on a piecey, a short distance away. On being quizzed where Cliffy the Jacobite and Big Flatters were, he explained how they had retreated due to the serious avalanche danger, but he had decided to continue, as he was so far up and reasoned he may have triggered one himself while descending.

'Ya didna come across some lunatic climber while ya wir up here, did ya? We seen a crackpot oot on the face o' Stob Coire nam Beith.'

'Eh, that wiz me,' he laughed. 'Totally shitin' ma breeks! The only safe route wiz tae stick tae the hard sna' an' ice an' head oot onta the face. Ma legs are stull shakin' yit.'

The wolves rounded on him and ripped him mercilessly with the usual black humour, but highly commended him for his choice of 'safe route'. While they delved into their own food supplies, Sandy, who was a newcomer to the club, nonchalantly enquired if anyone had a screwdriver on them as his crampons didn't fit his boots and they would most definitely be needed for the steep descent to the bealach (pass) between Stob Coire nan Lochan.

Quick as a flash, Frankie was on to it, 'Eh, hud on son, ehl jist hae a wee rummage in ma toolbox here. Ehv got a hammer, eh, a junior hacksaw, a plane an' a sander but ehm clean oot o' screwdrivers, sorry.' The others duly fell about laughing. This was always the case. There were never any prisoners taken when someone made a balls-up or said the wrong thing. Thankfully, one lad had a little screwdriver on a Swiss army knife and the crampons were fitted to Sandy's boots, which was just as well for the descent to the bealach was challenging down steep snow and ice. The situation got worse as they dropped off into the corrie on the west side. A wind-blasted, hard packed wall of snow, interspersed with rocky outcrops, welcomed them into its jaws. Bodies were scattered all over the face, each man warily searching for the safest line, and at one point, Charlie lost a crampon, which took off down the slope. As bad as the situation was, again he was afforded no sympathy and told to 'toughen up an' git on wi' it'.

At length, they made it down to safety and all fears and apprehensions from the day's trials were soon forgotten at the bottom of many pint glasses in the Clachaig bar that night.

The Bothy Fire

In the caald glens o' Scotland, you lie dormant, still an' dead
A phoenix in a shallow grave, wahr silent wings await their spread
Longin' fir the spark o' life, that builds a roarin' flame
The dragon's voice can sing once mair, an' grace the cosy hame
Devourin' lumps o' black gold, an' peat fae lonely hags
Wahr nature's finest rule the roost, the wildcat, eagle an' stag
Yiv feasted on Scots pine, her resin smell so sweet
An' ither wood o' grandeur, providin' us wi' heat

Which brings us on tae man, yir tool fir gittin' started
You need him an' he needs you, baith can never be parted
Yiv witnessed many passin' through, an' many that huv stayed
They've sung the sangs o Hamish Imlach, ah the way tae Slade
Yiv heard ower many chanters, some could fill a hall
An' ithers that wir chorus cats, screechin' oot thir call
Yiv watched men metamorphisize, inta drunkaholic demons
An' banshees cursin' all in sight, wah used tae pass fir weemin

Yiv warmed up politicians – doctors, shrinks an' fools
An' laughed as drunken socialites, huv tumbled aff thir stools
Yiv seen the Jekyll's turn tae Hyde's, sat ringside at a brawl
Wahr black-eyed champs stood undefeated, an' losers had tae crawl
Yiv heard elite mountaineers, tell tales o' fearless climbs
An' listened tae Billy Liar's fibs, a hunder thoosand times
Yiv watched the tears fall fae men's eyes, cryin' fir comrades fallen
An' crooners serenadin' malt, wi' sangs that wir appallin'

Yiv nearly choked the company, wi' fumes o' toxic death
An' forced incompetent fire starters, ootside quick fir breath
Yiv hud yir hearth ower-burdened, an' set yir lum ablaze
An' watched the headless chickens panic, when the bothy nearly razed
Yiv hud yir belly tickled, wi' tough, asbestos hands
When garments aff the washin' line, fell in yir white-hot palms
Yiv been asked tae produce miracles, wi' waste that widna light
But ither nights yiv burned like Hell, twa hunder Fahrenheit

Yiv witnessed scenes so farcical, as yir embers slowly died
When a perty's fuel pile ran a drought, an' the fire master cried
Yiv seen a clan o amadans, tear up the bothy flair
Destroyin' the shrine o' Ossian, in a mindless vandal's snare
Valhalla they will never see, when karma has her way
A Sigrun-led Valkyrie charge, tae slay the helpless prey
An' wut aboot the ither lot, the anes that leave their crap
A sentence deep inside Hell's gut, would mak the bugger's flap

Yiv seen some culinary disasters, fae chefs ill-trained an' raw
A pot o' CJD cuisine, which the makers thought wiz braw
Meatballs, beans an' rogan josh, an' a layer o' rabbit's shite
A time bomb tickin' in thir bowels, yir spark could soon ignite
Yiv watched precarious bivvy tins, balancin' on a stove
Then seen it ah cowped on the deck, chef's temper primed tae hove
An' there upon yir mantlepiece, a solitary candle burns
An icon in a whisky bottle, the tickin' wax hand turns

Yir cracklin' voice has mellowed now, an' all but gone tae sleep
An' the phoenix hibernates once mair, into her cinder keep
Yir final plumes o' smoke, huv dispersed way doon the glen
An' kissed the heather blanket, that courts a mountain Ben
The circus lies in slumber, in a pre-hangover daze
Oot afore yir flame wiz spent, an' yir criticizin' gaze
An' nae doubt that's no' ah, yiv witnessed doon the years
But they'll be back an' you'll be back, tae warm friends an' peers.

CHAPTER 5

Carry on Camping (Part 1)

Sourlies bothy

THROUGHOUT THE EARLIER history of the club, the preferred choice of accommodation for weekenders had mostly been rough camping, with the odd bothy meet thrown in for a wee variation and certainly a lot more comfortable when the weather turned, as Scottish weather often does. But the weather was never really an issue for those wishing to get out for a few nights under canvas, whether it was howling gales, horizontal rain, raging blizzards or swarms of cavernous midges and by the 1980s, a regular and committed band of real drinking characters formed the nucleus of a new breed, some of whom had become involved in the growing popularity of climbing all of the Munros.

(Most readers will be familiar with the term 'Munro bagging', but for those who are not, a Munro is a Scottish mountain with a height of 3,000 ft (914.4 m) or over and the first list was compiled by Sir Hugh Munro in 1891 and published in the Scottish

Mountaineering Club's Journal, numbering 283 in total. This total has since varied as heights have been re-measured throughout the years, fluctuating anywhere between 277 and 284, with the current total sitting at 282.)

The club was very kindly funded on a yearly basis from the NCR business, so much so that a number of brand new Vango Force Ten tents were purchased for use by members. These were two, three and four-man tents, which, through the coming years, would often see many more bodies in them than was specified, especially the bigger ones which came to be affectionately known as 'the party tents'. This was where the after hours drinking sessions would continue when last orders had been called at the local bar and someone would produce a bottle of whisky, or anything fitting an alcoholic description, to be passed around into the 'wee sma' oors'. These tents took more punishment than some of Mike Tyson's opponents and really lived up to their name of 'Force Ten', more than capable of withstanding the wildest of weather or party. It is a true testament to a quality product when the company 'Blacks of Greenock' are still selling these almost invincible pieces of kit, and one or two members still regularly use these tents nearly 50 years after purchase.

A common problem which repeated itself many times over the years was finding a suitable location on which to pitch a group of tents. This was made all the more difficult, especially following the mandatory extended pub stop and then arriving in a completely new area in pitch darkness. There were numerous occasions when morning dawned, tent flaps would zip open, a head like a burst mattress would pop out like a drunken tortoise from a shell and greet the new day with a cry of, 'Wahr the bliddee hell are we?'

Absolute paramount to the decision on the said location was that it had to be within fair walking distance to the boozer, but more importantly, with a manageable stagger back to the tents later on. This was taken to the utmost extremes during one weekend when the destination was Fort William. The minibus pulled in at the popular and lively Commando Bar in Spean Bridge to let members out for a stretch of the legs and a light refreshment. The inevitable Friday night feeling kicked in as men justified throwing as many pints and nips down their necks following 'a hard week's graft', while the laughter got louder and the mood became wilder. The driver had had enough and called time before the legion of drunkards could cross the Rubicon.

'Right, that is it, ya bums! Drink up pronto an' git yir erses back on the bus!'

After much press ganging and cajoling, the last man finally boarded the bus, only for Davie San to announce that he was getting off and planning to march over the Grey Corries and would see them in Fort Bill tomorrow. He grabbed his tent and pack, then watched as the bus disappeared into the night. The next morning, he awoke, got the gas burner on for a brew and went out to stretch his legs (no doubt bursting for a pee) and was greeted by a sight, which nearly knocked him on his back. There, only yards in front of him, was the headquarters for Spean Bridge's Finest – the local police station!

In his drunken stupor the previous night, he had decided that the lovely patch of well-maintained, almost bowling green-like grass he had 'found' would be an excellent place to erect his tent. This was, in fact, the common ground outside the pub, and situated literally in the front garden of the cop shop. One can only imagine what the big sergeant's reaction would have been while yawning and opening the curtains, to find a dishevelled vagabond pishing on his lawn. It was time for a sharp exit.

Johnny V Diff remembered one of his earliest meets up near Coulags in the north-west and a fine camping spot for the group just off the A890 road. A lovely morning dawned on the Saturday, and the lads wasted no time in picking off the Munros to the north of Achnashellach. On return, however, their glorious day turned into a nightmare as they found a few tons of dead fish had been dumped intentionally or unintentionally near the campsite. The putrid stench was overpowering, but tough as old boots, they endured the horrendous guff before beating a hasty retreat the next morning.

July was a historically quiet month for the club as some members headed off on holidays with families, loved ones or friends, and so it was a small but enthusiastic group who trundled north on the

A9 while The Corries belted out from the cassette player and the pile of empties from the carry out grew substantially larger. The destination was Inchnadamph, way up in the stunningly rugged and picturesque landscape of Assynt, Sutherland, where the party would be tackling the Munros of Conival and Beinn Mhòr Asaint.

'Driver, any chance of those among us who are parched, partaking in a small libation in a local hostelry in Ullapool?' (This was always an unfortunate scenario for the designated driver on weekenders who had to not only remain professionally sober but also put up with the deteriorating rabble and friendly abuse which raged around them.) The 'small libation', of course, went to chucking out time at 1.00am and may have gotten completely out of hand with offers to attend a local party, had it not been for stone-cold sober Wee Ecky's excellent man-management skills as a driver. 'Fir Christ's sake, wull yiz git on that fuckin' bus afore eh laive every single ane o yiz behind!'

The poor driver was afforded no respite, and the nightmare continued for the next 24 miles or so amid a cacophony of shouting, laughter and hollered requests.

'Turn The Corries up, there's the 'Rattlin' Bog' on.'

'Anybody got a spare tin o' swally?'

'Driver, any chance o' a pish stop?'

The minibus headlights finally located a single track road past the village of Inchnadamph, and they turned down, hoping to find some decent ground. A little further, they came to what looked like a suitable site and stumbled off, giggling and cursing as they tried to find personal gear with head torches being the main priority. The glowing eyes of cattle were spotted a short distance away, giving concern for a few of the would-be campers as a tent placed on top of a freshly laid cowpat would not end well, especially when rolling it away later. Dougie Mac climbed over a nearby dry-stone dyke and called to the others, 'Here lads, this is perfect. Home sweet home fir the night. Throw ah the gear ower.'

On closer inspection, and helped by the beam of a torchlight, Dougie was told in no uncertain terms where to go. 'Yir in a bliddee GRAVEYAIRD ya muppet!'

The sinner did sleep in the enclave of the dead that night while those on the outside, being in such close proximity to a burial ground, spent sleepless hours wondering if the ghosts would drag them underground or, more worryingly, if a large, clumsy coo tripped on their tent and squashed them to death.

The morning light shed some clue as to where they had pitched up the previous night, slap bang in the vicinity of the Old Parish Church and the centuries old burial ground for the Macleod clan of Assynt. The smell of a fry-up wafted over from the graveyard as Dougie Mac held court with the Macleod ghosts, no doubt arguing over who was getting what from the sizzling pan. It is worth a little mention of the epic that followed later that day on the mountains, once the camp was struck. Conival fell first to the marauding band, then a successful assault of Beinn Mhòr Asaint completed the goals for the day. However, what should have been an easy enough descent turned into a monumental calamity. The sensible option would have been to retrace the route, but the group fancied a sporting challenge and tackled the narrow ridge to the South Top.

Careful analysis of the excellent *The Munros: Scottish Mountaineering Club Hillwalkers' Guide Volume One* clearly states, 'A direct descent from the South Top to Dubh Loch Mor is not advised.' As no one had a copy on them to carefully analyse the route, a 'direct descent' it was, but only after Dougie Mac informed them that he had found a scree run (small broken rocks and stones) that would 'have them at the bottom in no time at all'.

(This was a situation that would be repeated fairly regularly over the years and was infamously labelled 'Dougie Mac's Tours' where extreme danger and possible death were high on the agenda. Rather hilariously, he ended up on one of his own tours whilst tackling The Saddle in Glen Shiel when the club was on a meet to Kintail and camped at Loch Duich. The great man would admit he was never one to bother with the technicalities of a map and compass and much preferred 'gut instinct'. As a thick mist descended on the ridge, this trusty gut instinct led him to follow a line of pylons down to a loch. Unfortunately, this wasn't the familiar Loch Duich but that of Loch Hourn! Dougie had gone completely south of north and ended up on a marathon hitch-hike back to the Kintail

Lodge Hotel, where he duly arrived to find his friends blootered and falling out of the door as the bar was now closed. On missing a much hoped for pint, it is said that his bottom lip was bigger than the navigation balls-up he'd had on the hill that day.)

Spirits were high as they whooped and laughed while flying down the slope, but just as Dougie was about to be congratulated on a brilliant choice of route, the fun evaporated, and they were forced into an abrupt stop. The scree run had petered out and was about to deposit the group over a cliff. The ground was incredibly steep, interspersed with wet grass and huge crags. Again, the simple solution was to retrace the steps, but instead, it was a case of 'every man for themselves', scattered and desperately clinging on to clumps of heather and loose rock, trying to find a way down that didn't involve death.

Dougie Mac had miraculously raced down like a demented dervish and stood at the loch howling with laughter as one by one, men stumbled in looking like they had just come from a chicken run through Hades. The fear written on their faces soon turned to apprehensive smiles, then shared laughter as each man recounted his own personal battle for survival on the mountain. All except for one that is as still high up and clinging motionless to a large outcrop with a waterfall cascading down it was 'Crack o' Dawn' Colin. Naturally, the rest down below thought this was hilarious. As Dougie had led the party into this hell, it was he who had to climb back up and coax their stricken friend to safety. There were certainly no cattle or ghosts to worry about that night and indeed the only spirits doing the rounds were those of the malt variety being merrily downed in the safe and cosy confines of an Ullapool bar.

Torridon, way over in the north-west, was a place which grew popular with the club in the 1980s and for obvious reasons. The landscape could rival the best in Scotland for choice of mountains, many of which have some of the oldest rock formations on the planet. The chosen site for rough camping on these early meets was right in front of the Youth Hostel, but no one locally seemed to mind. On this particular meet, there was to be no summits conquered as the weather was truly horrendous and chucking it down in buckets. A low level walk around the bulking mass of Liathach at least gave some sense of achievement for a journey so far from home.

With a good helping of food in the bellies and bivvy tins washed, it was time for the Saturday night shenanigans in the Loch Torridon Hotel, which was situated a fair distance from the tents. The quickest route there was to cut across the bay rather than follow the road around, and a few keen revellers had already taken this option earlier on when it was still daylight. The Gibb Brothers were in full voice as the songs belted out and the ale flowed as quickly as the burns were flowing outside. Following 'last orders', bodies staggered out into the darkness with no head torches, flailing around trying to gather their bearings and choose the right direction to the tents.

Geordie F and Davie G were guttered and propping each other up as they unsteadily followed the white line along the road. They remembered the path left the road and ran parallel with the burn. What they didn't remember, however, was that the path took a dogleg turn to get to the campsite. Both men went headfirst, straight into the freezing, cold burn. Davie was holding Geordie under by the chest as he desperately scrambled to get some leverage. When they did manage to get out, Geordie was short of a hearing aid and a pair of contact lenses, which Davie thought was hilarious.

Disaster befell two other unfortunate characters that night. Thommo and Slambo were two of the party who earlier had crossed the bay as the crow flies. What they failed to remember was that Upper Loch Torridon is a sea loch and therefore tidal. They too had come out of the pub steaming drunk and into the darkness, staggered to an embankment to return by the same route earlier and jumped straight into the welcoming seawater. When the drookit pair made it back to the campsite, they fell over some newcomer's tent who was on his first NCR meet and flattened it, bending all the poles in the process. The poles were replaced by the club, but the poor lad was never seen on a meet again.

Geordie F seemed to have an uncanny knack for plunging into burns and rivers, and drink wasn't always the reason. Many years back, the club used to camp near a cottage in Glencoe, where an arrangement worked well with the owner and a half bottle of whisky found its way into his pocket each visit. Geordie was heading for Bidean nam Bian one morning but couldn't resist falling into a burn as he crossed and smashed his watch to pieces.

His most impressive diving stunt by far was on a bitterly cold winter's morning in the western Cairngorms. Having just departed Ruigh Aiteachain bothy, he was heading with others for the nearby Munros of Mullach Clach a' Bhlàir and Sgòr Gaoithe when they were presented with a challenging river crossing, made all the more difficult as the rocks above the water were glazed with a coating of ice.

The rest successfully passed the test and made it over without any mishaps, then waited for old 'Twinkle Toes' while offering words of encouragement. These fell on a dodgy hearing aid, however, as the first gingerly planted boot shot off the rock and sent poor Geordie into an acrobatic concoction of involuntary moves skywards. Gravity brought him down quickly with an eye-catching belly flop, which was perfectly executed to produce maximum splash. The riverbank judges had no hesitation in awarding straight 10s before they collapsed in a mangled heap of hilarity. Completely soaked to the bone, he waded over and, without the slightest complaint, said, 'Ach, ehl jist crack on lads, the claes wull dry aff once eh git going.'

Astounded by his statement and knowing that the thermometer had already recorded -8c before any wind chill, his pals persuaded him to return and put dry kit on. This he did, and hard as nails, he eventually caught the young tigers up to lead and break trail for them through deep snow.

Geordie F could probably have given Davie San a run for his money when it came to disastrous episodes. One such incident happened in the old Forfar club bothy of Whitehaugh in Glen Clova. He was leaning over a candle, trying to grab some light and take out a contact lens when he heard a strange crackling noise. He turned to Fred and said, 'That's some heavy rain battering on the roof.'

Rather concerned, Fred replied, 'That's no RAIN, ya daft erse, yir bloody hair's on FIRE!'

Geordie's natural perm was ablaze but quickly extinguished by a flurry of patting, panicking hands, courtesy of the newly self-appointed fire-fighters in the room.

Now back to the camping and sticking with the water theme. The days of mass camping near the official site at Kintail finally came to an end when the club were banned from using the ground. Fast forward a few years, and an alternative pitch was found on the shores of Loch Duich, which had the added bonus of being much nearer to the Kintail Lodge Hotel. Charlie had spent his first visit to the mountain Mecca climbing the magnificent Five Sisters in blazing sunshine with mouthwatering views in every direction he turned. With feelings of sheer elation and exhilaration, the Bonnie Prince had put on a pace, descending quickly and looking to get his food scoffed sharpish, changed into his dancing gear and shot along to the boozer for a celebratory dozen pints.

In his haste to put up his tent on the Friday night, he maybe should have clocked where the older heads were pitching theirs, far higher than any last piece of seaweed. Standing at the bar, the Bonnie Prince surveyed the lively scene around him, friends laughing, the guy in the corner giving it laldy on the guitar and two inebriated locals arguing over whose round it was. As the creamy head of a fresh pint caressed his lips, Mikey Fitz (who had been enjoying a pre-pub kip) entered the bar some time later, ordered a pint, then turned to Charlie and said quite matter-of-factly in his warm southern Irish accent, 'By the way, yir tent's in the loch.'

'Ach awa an' shite! Yir pullin' ma leg. Are ya?'

The Bonnie Prince bolted out the door and broke the 100 metres world sprint record back along the track, just to see if the deadpan Irishman was in fact pulling his leg. He wasn't. The bright orange apex of the tent stood solitary and proud in 2 ft of gently lapping and steadily rising sea water. Now, as highly waterproof as the Force Ten range is, not even Moses himself lying in there was gonna hold back the incoming tide. Charlie unzipped the door flaps to find his gear floating around like a child's toys in a bath and had to move into rapid rescue mode while a short but dry distance away, a newly arrived audience of 'friends' gathered to shout words of encouragement through tears of laughter.

Having to move a tent once erected and settled is never a

pleasant task, especially in the dark and when flooding is involved, but for one member, his tent was very nearly carried off against his wishes. Like nearly every time before, the long journeys north and west from Dundee (including alcoholic beverage stops) meant the hour was late, and frequently into the wee small hours of the morning when tents were finally pitched. When blootered drunk, pitch-darkness and swarms of midges combine, then the choice of ground is sometimes overlooked in favour of getting the damn thing up swiftly.

Some years ago and way before the area became engulfed in a commercial tsunami of tourism, when one could freely and without health and safety issues, climb the monument to commemorate the 1745 Raising of the Jacobite Standard, Geordie F was guilty of all of the above outdoor crimes while camped on a meet under the historic and majestic Glenfinnan railway viaduct (now alternatively known by many as the 'Harry Potter bridge' from the famed film series). At around 3.00am he awoke with a tickly sensation all over the parts of his body, which hadn't made it inside the sleeping bag, which was nearly ALL. After fumbling around, he found his trusty old Petzl head torch and switched it on to a scene of horror. He had inadvertently pitched on top of an anthill, which had pissed off the chief commander ant, who in turn ordered his army of ten squillion to 'attack'. They didn't even have to force entry as the occupier had left the flaps open and in they poured. Thoughts of 'Rorke's Drift', 'The Alamo' and 'Custer's Last Stand' flooded through Geordie's mind as he shrieked, screamed and shook his way to safety and a new pitch.

Glenfinnan was to become a regular meet and a firm favourite with the club, not solely due to the free camping in the stunning location of Loch Shiel, or the vast array of rugged mountains to climb, or even the welcoming local watering holes in the nearby hotels, all of which did tick the boxes, but the added attraction of the annual Gathering and Highland Games each August was a big pull.

Wee Balbirnie wasn't a regular club member, but once every so often, he would attend a meet and usually make a complete arse of himself, which was a truly impressive achievement given the company he was in and who were known to like a wee bevvy or ten themselves. Wee Balbirnie's problem was that he couldn't hold his drink. He was the kind of guy who would turn up at the NCR car park on a Friday night to board the minibus armed with two litres of the infamous Buckfast wine and proceed to steam through it with a passion. I don't think he ever set foot on a mountain, but he sure as hell set foot on some people's toes.

While men had been marching over the challenging terrain on Sgùrr Thuilm and Sgùrr nan Coireachan, Wee Balbirnie had been wading through pints at the Glenfinnan Games and was extremely pished when the mountain men returned to the campsite. Focus was placed on getting changed pronto and firing up the gas stoves for food in readiness for the evening's ceilidh at the Gathering. The mood was tranquil, peaceful and content among the huddle of tents, complemented almost therapeutically by the steady murmur of gas jets and the odd piece of cutlery stirring some culinary delight in a bivvy tin.

Suddenly, all hell broke loose in tent three, where Wee Balbirnie was sharing with Mackie.

'Ya stupid wee bastard! Yiv melted a hole in ma jeckit! Git oot o' here afore eh kill ya!'

It was in Wee Balbirnie's best interests to vacate the tent immediately, as the said jacket was no run-of-the-mill garment but a very expensive leather one, now complete with ventilation. The wee man was walking a tightrope, and, in his drunken stupor, it didn't take long before he fell off, straight onto Dougie Mac's tent and caved it in. Once Dougie had managed to untangle himself from inside the wreckage, he sought out the guilty man and administered the punishment in the form of a swift right hander. BANG! Wee Balbirnie burst into tears, which was met with lots of sympathy from his fellow campers.

This would be the absolute point when the perpetrator of such acts of lunacy would retire to the sleeping bag with their tail between their legs for a long, hard think, but Wee Balbirnie was made of much more idiotic mettle than the average man. The first notes from the band began to fill the air and signalled the start of the ceilidh in the packed Gathering tent. Fred had just joined the others, all spruced up with his first pint in hand looking forward to a few Strip The Willows and Canadian Barn Dances later when, from out of nowhere lurched the small frame of Wee Balbirnie who tripped and spilt a whole pint of stout down Fred's jeans. The one-man-riot was placed on Death Row while Fred had to forget any ambitions of burning up the dance floor with any birling or jigging for the simple fact, he looked like he had pished his breeks.

There were of course the very rare occasions when an official campsite was used, purely for the reason that a pub or pubs were situated nearby. Fort William wasn't an area renowned for quiet, rough camping locations due to the simple fact that the place was, and still is, heaving with bodies. The club used to wild camp in Glen Nevis across from the official site, something which would be totally frowned upon and unthinkable these days. Four members had signed up for the charity event 'Boots Across Scotland' some years ago and were looking for some place to camp as near to Fort William's centre as they could. They found the ideal place, or so they thought, which may or may not have been official but said 'CAMPING' on the gateway, so in they drove and unloaded the gear from the two cars. They noticed that there were no other tents around or any sign of a Reception but carried on regardless.

Big Betty had brought his ancient 'Continental' tent from the 1970s, which was emptied from the large bag with aluminium poles and pegs scattered all over the place as the men tried to figure out how to erect it. As heads were scratched and chins were rubbed and faces wore a look of utter confusion, the small group were startled when a character came ranting and raging towards them, screaming 'you can't just turn up and throw a bloody tent up here!'

All innocent protests were forcefully shot down by the very angry and rude man, so the lads packed up and got back into their cars. The lovely lawn, however, was sodden with rainwater, and as they attempted to drive off, the wheels churned up huge channels of mud, spraying chunks of once bonnie turf everywhere. Both rear mirrors were by now filled by some wildly animated maniac who was doing a war dance while the vehicles made their escape as swiftly as they could.

On the subject of sharing a tent, it is vitally important that all dwellers get along with each other, respect each other's space and share some common rules for in-house tidiness and cleanliness. This can, however, fall apart completely when campers have been involved in a heavy bevvy session in the pub. In the sometimes claustrophobic confines of a small tent, all campers should be able to breathe fresh oxygen and not be subjected to reckless and indiscriminate farting, but it does go on. One of the major problems encountered is being absolutely bursting for a toilet, especially when the weather is horrendous outside and the thought of going out to pee bollock-naked in the pitch-black darkness in a howling gale, horizontal rain or arctic frost is enough to break the toughest of folk.

Then again, there were some who followed a different plan altogether (or no plan at all). In the aftermath of yet another round of Clachaig shenanigans, Frankie and Wee Ecky retired to their two-man Vango and quickly collapsed into deep slumber. Well, that was until Frankie was rudely awakened by his inebriated companion.

'Aw, yir pishin' ah ower is, ya wee shite!'

'Uuuuuugh,' came the grunted reply as the wee man continued to soak his buddy, completely unaware he hadn't made it outside the tent.

Sometimes finding the head torch to find the front door to find the zip on the said door is nigh on impossible, and such was the case when Tardy and Big Betty had borrowed a tent from the latter's in-laws for a club meet to Skye. The tent itself had had some alterations by Big Betty's mother-in-law in the form of an 'inner extension wall' being sewn in at the 'head' end to allow for more room. Both men returned to the tent guttered after the usual drunken carnage in the Sligachan Hotel, and within a matter of minutes were off to the Land of Nod and snoring like a pair of clapped-out bulldozers. Sometime later, Big Betty awoke with a bladder at bursting point and somewhat disorientated, he began faking around in the dark, desperately trying to find the zip and the exit to 'urinal Shangri-La'.

The threat of pishing his breeks was about to surpass DEFCON 1 when his fingers grabbed onto a little corner of material, which he began pulling at like a man possessed. Tardy awoke to the sound of a large 'Rrrrrrip!' followed by more ripping and shredding.

'Betty, wut the hell are ya daein?'

'Eh need tae git oot, ehm gonna pish masel!'

'The door's at the ITHER end, ya numpty!'

The big man didn't even reply as he burrowed his way out under the flysheet, leaving a trail of tattered and torn material in his wake. The new extension was no more.

Some of the more switched-on members have avoided being caught in any of these previous calamitous scenarios by wisely having a 'pee bottle' near to hand, much like the old bedpans of yesteryear. Andy Ran Dan and Neily were two characters well known for climbing hard, playing hard and drinking harder. For them, any vessel which could hold pish and thus avoid having to go out into the night was fair game. Unfortunately, this information wasn't always relayed between the pals.

The club was based at the old campsite in Portnalong, Skye and on the Friday night arrival had indulged in a throat-oiling session in the nearby Taigh Ailean Hotel. Ran Dan and Neily had staggered back to their two-man tent and were soon bagged up and counting sheep. Through the night, Ran Dan had awakened with the familiar signs of too much liquid in the system and had managed to grasp a large pot, which he filled and then emptied outside the tent. Little was remembered of the night's shenanigans as small groups tackled various summits in the Cuillin.

A strenuous day builds a strenuous appetite, and the aforementioned pair waded through a mountain of pasta served up from a large pot. It was around halfway through their demolishing of the scran that Ran Dan recalled having to pee in a pot through the night. He said nothing until Neily had swallowed his last piece of swirly pasta. Not one to mince his words, Neily commented to the chef that the food was sub-standard and actually 'pretty pish'.

Chef Ran Dan paused for a few seconds, then agreed with his friend, blaming it on the 'cheap crap sauce fae Asda,' before adding, 'That wiz the pot eh pished in last night an' forgot to clean it.'

Neily's reply cannot be shown due to the extreme nature of the wording.

CARRY ON CAMPING (PART 1)

The camping calamities were many, so for now, we shall pack up the tent poles and pegs, roll away the fly sheet and inner and return later for some more pitched episodes of madness.

The Sourlies Moose

Sourlies bothy so tranquil an' serene
Return is a must once sampled an' seen
Fir a better settin' nae man could ask
Wahr rare sunny days allow ya tae bask
But ane such visit fir three mountaineers
Damn nearly reduced ane o' the hardmen tae tears
The culprit? A furry wee brither o' Mickey
Cheeky an' impudent an' boy wiz he tricky

The lads sat comfy recallin' stories of old
While guzzlin' doon drams o' the heavenly gold
A bonnie evenin' fir sure tae pass on the lawn
Watchin' the last o' the sunshine slowly withdrawin'
Then in the doorway there appeared a wee moose
Broad shiddered an' brazen like HE owned the hoose
Big Betty observed then eez chin he did rub
'See that lang-tailed devil, he's efter oor grub!'

Nae 'To A Moose' friendly terms wir laid
Big Betty leapt up an' grabbed the spade
That rodent wiz chased ah aroond the room
By a madman attemptin' tae seal eez doom
The smart wee creature darted this way then that
An' dodged all attempts tae render him flat
Ootside, the lads wir fallin' aboot
As the wee moose outwitted the fumin' galoot

'Sit yirsel doon man an' hae anither malt
Yiv invaded HIS hoose, itz ah YOUR fault!'
Big Betty sat doon but couldna relax
While the moose laughed merrily behind their backs
Now, if you should enter this fortress domain
Yid better git doon tae some serious prayin'
Best tak an offerin' o' biscuits an' cheese
An' hope the wee chancer is happily appeased.

This poetic pantomime occurred during a mini tour of the Knoydart bothies when three club members enjoyed a period of glorious Spring weather some years ago. Sourlies, which sits in the stunning location near the head of Loch Nevis, welcomed the trio into her abode following a big day on the ridge along to Sgùrr na Cìche with heavily laden packs. Little did they know, a wee (but huge in stature) furry 'door-mouse' awaited their arrival demanding food with menaces.

CHAPTER 6

The Yellow Submarine

Getting there

THE SUBJECT OF transport and how to get to mountain locations has been covered in previous chapters, where anything from a hearse-like conversion to an old ambulance to a 52-seater coach was used, as long as it got the club to its chosen destination.

As the weekend numbers dropped off from the days of the big coaches, much of the 1980s was a time of change and hunting high and low for suitable minibuses to hire. Someone who knew someone knew a guy locally who had a minibus and hired it out, which fitted the bill for the lads just dandy. He was contacted, and yes, the club could have the bus for the weekend.

Geordie F had gone up to his house to pick it up on the Friday night, but the owner wasn't in. And there was a dilemma. There were two buses in the driveway, one of which Geordie thought looked like an ambulance or an ice cream van. He paused, then remembered the owner had said it was 'a high-roofed vehicle and the keys would be in it,' so he reckoned it must be the bigger one.

'Aw ya dancer,' thought Geordie, 'this is the dog's bollocks.'

The plush 23-seater kicked into life and was soon on its way to pick up the group at the NCR factory car park. The dozen or so men assembled there couldn't believe their eyes as Geordie rolled up beside them.

'Hey, this is arite eh? Wahr did ya steal it fae?'

'Diz it hae a TV an' video recorder on board?'

'Mair importantly, diz it hae a free bar on board?'

Geordie was bombarded with wisecracks as the men loaded in the gear and made themselves probably the most comfortable they had ever been on a meet, which for this rough and ready bunch was used to, was ample and luxurious surroundings. Spirits were high as the bus headed north to the much-loved Glen Clova area, but a nightmare scenario soon materialised at Kirriemuir where the bus needed to be fuelled up. The high roof presented all sorts of problems when getting it into the pump, but with some tricky manoeuvring, they got her filled up and were on their jolly way up the glen. Summits were won, beers and fine malts were sunk, and much laughter and storytelling were shared in the Clova Hotel climber's bar round a roaring, open fire.

As Geordie pulled up at the owner's house late Sunday afternoon, he was already excitedly going over what he was going to say, how fantastic and comfortable the bus had been and that the club would definitely be looking to hire it on a monthly basis. However, that is not how this little story ended. The front door of the house flew open and out stormed an irate owner, foaming at the mouth and filling the garden air with volleys of four-letter words which exploded in the face of the baffled driver. It took more than a few moments before Geordie's hearing aid was able to decipher some sense and understand why the man was so angry. It turned out that he had taken the wrong bus, the very bus which the guy had needed for an important passenger contract that weekend and had spent much of Friday night racing up and down the Kingsway looking for his bus and a driver to strangle. Worse still, he had had to get one from Edinburgh to carry out the work. Needless to say, Geordie never managed to deliver his glowing speech and ask about next month's availability.

Prior to the club finally securing a regular monthly hire with a reputable company for the weekend meets, it was Davie San who found a solution to the problem of transport. He had a friend who had a minibus and, for very good 'mate's rates', the deal was done. The word minibus, however, was maybe a bit of an ambitious description as this mobile heap of junk was more akin to a place in the starting line-up of the 1960s cartoon series *The Wacky Races*. The era of 'The Yellow Submarine' was about to begin. To keep things in perspective, though, the club had not ditched the mountains for new adventures of underwater maritime mischief. It was the handle given to the yellow vehicle, which could seat 12 bodies uncomfortably, squeeze in a mountain of gear and generally break down when farthest away from Dundee.

The old warhorse did, in fact, provide many memorable weekends. Covering places far and wide to the north and west, she always managed to roll back into the NCR car park at some point on a Sunday night, with times varying considerably. During one forgettable journey, acrid black smoke was billowing out from somewhere and finding its way inside, whether through the dashboard or a hole in the floor and straight into everyone's lungs. Tough mountain men were complaining of nearly choking to death and thick lumps of 'black stuff' coming from their noses.

On another occasion, they had travelled to Inchnadamph way up in Sutherland when the water pump decided to pack in. A few of the lads jumped aboard on the Saturday morning, leaving the rest behind, and with numerous stops to let the engine cool down, they slowly made their way to Ullapool, where they found a garage minutes before it was about to close at midday. By a huge stroke of luck, the guy had a spare water pump and had the old submarine back in operation in no time, which was just as well or the stranded band at Inchnadamph may have went into outright mutiny.

The final meet, which ended the stormy and at times volatile relationship between the club and the crippled vessel, was during an intended trip to Applecross, way up in the north-west of Scotland. The sing-songs, bevvying and joviality began to wane amongst the crew as the sub began to struggle, and maximum speed went down to a flat-out 10mph. With a cough and a splutter, the minibus staggered into the small village of Lochcarron and then ground to a halt. The hour was very late as the disgruntled and cursing mob departed, then set about looking for a suitable campsite. The perfect pitch was found beside some tables and benches, and shortly afterwards, all was calm again in sleepy Lochcarron, save for the sound of some bulldozer snoring and thunderous farts.

Any chance of a long lie was rudely disrupted by the local Boys in Blue, who kindly but assertively informed the vagrants that camping in a family picnic area was not the done thing in these parts and could they shift their arses out pronto! This was done and a new spot was found on the outskirts of the village. Then the small matter of trying to find a mechanic became all consuming. A kind local man agreed to have a look, and with a few bangs, clunks and shudders, he got the old lady ticking over again while informing the group that there seemed to be some problem with fuel blockage. The answer to this was to go and give the Submarine a little trial spin – up the Bealach na Bà, only one of the steepest and unrelenting roads with hairpin bends in the whole land! Incredibly, she passed the test and made it unscathed (or so they thought) back to Lochcarron.

Sunday morning dawned, and with hangovers buried and the campsite struck, the group boarded the minibus with some trepidation and a genuine worry that they may not get far and have to walk back to Dundee. The thought was too huge to digest and more than one man was heard cracking open a breakfast tin of ale. They hadn't gone far when the inevitable spluttering and jolting returned, and a few complaints rained down from the rear that they had almost spilled their beer.

Dougie Mac, who it's fair to say was no stranger to tinkering with engines himself, lifted up the bonnet, had a scratch of his head, a rub of the chin, then, following some complicated mathematical equations, worked out the answer. A large plastic, empty water bottle was used to syphon diesel into, then with some jiggery-pokery and tying with boot laces, a set-up was fashioned where the vehicle got moving again. This lasted around 20 miles until the process had to be repeated all over again. 'Crack o' Dawn Colin' (the chief syphoning engineer) had swallowed so much diesel that he was beginning to move quicker than the bus. His lips were burnt and blistered, but to a man of his standing, this was just like another night on the drink.

By the time they reached Bonnie Dundee, the cows from the famous saying 'until the cows come home' had already been home ages ago. Men stumbled from the bus with huge beards and no recollection of what month it was. In all seriousness, though, it was a journey of epic hell. And the Yellow Submarine? It was last seen being scuttled in the River Tay while all members of The Beatles (living and dead) were ceremoniously cursed.

CHAPTER 7

The Ghillies

Shenavall bothy

FOR ANY REGULAR visitors to the mountains and glens of Scotland, whether it is to climb, walk, ramble, camp, mountain bike or fish, there is a high chance that at some point during their travels, they will cross paths and come into contact with a ghillie (or ghillies) working the land. The word derives from the Scottish Gaelic *gille*, meaning lad or servant, and in ancient times, they were the manservants of clan chieftains, attending to their needs and, in some cases, expected to carry them over burns and rivers.

The modern-day ghillie (or estate worker or gamekeeper) would no doubt baulk at the suggestion that they should carry the Laird or Lady of the estate over some burn or river. They do, however, have a much more extensive and varied role in land management on the vast estates covering anything and everything from deerstalking to managing fishing beats to guiding high-paying clients on sporting shoots.

The ongoing calls for a 'radical reform of the country's land ownership rules' continue along with arguments that the 'land monopoly which exists, gives landowners too much power' and in some cases is damaging to rural communities. The counter arguments may retort that millions of pounds come into the economy through sporting estates, but given that many of these are private (and some foreign owned) is the country really enjoying huge financial gains from this?

Problems arise for outdoor enthusiasts when these private estates start to discourage or try to force people to stay off 'their' land with fences and signs and the issue becomes contentious. The main word to abide by is 'respect' for the property and owner, and things should be fine and dandy, but occasionally, just occasionally, some 'rogue' ghillie police think they are Billy Big Bollocks and attempt to enforce their own laws. Thankfully, these incidents have been few and far between and mostly, there has been a mutual respect and even the odd bout of banter.

For many years, near the shores of Loch Laggan, Aberarder was a favourite area for rough camping giving excellent access to the Creag Mèagaidh group and the mountains to the south. On this particular meet the weather was truly horrendous and only a few of the hardiest lunatics had attempted to reach the high tops with absolutely no success.

The rest had wisely opted for the cosier surroundings of the Monadh Liath pub (sadly, no longer a public bar) beside the old, ruined church where things had developed into a full-blown drinking session. A local gamekeeper and his mate had been making serious efforts to reduce the levels of golden liquid in a few of the whisky bottles, and it wasn't long before Alex and Davie San had joined the pair for a right carry on. As the hours wore on and most of the company took the offer of a lift back to the campsite, the gamekeeper suggested continuing the whisky demolition back at his cottage. Alex and Davie needed no twisting of either arm and duly fell in with the tweed-clad pair. A few more drams had passed each man's lips when the gamekeeper cut the conversation abruptly, then boldly announced that 'things were getting boring' and it was 'time to liven the night up.'

He took a handful of 303 bullets from his pocket and launched them straight into the roaring fire. Now Alex was no spring chicken and borderline pished, but he still managed to depart his seat like a gazelle with a firework up its arse and exit through a nearby window with all the grace of an Olympic gymnast. He was taking absolutely no chances or hanging about to wait and see if he would be cut down in a hail of gunfire, a truly sad way to go, as he hadn't finished his dram. His mate, on the other hand, cackled and howled like a madman, taking great joy as each of the bullets exploded (although it has to be said that the bullets could thankfully not perform in their true sense without the gun).

Safety-conscious Alex bellowed through the window, 'San ya lunatic, save yirsel an' git oot o' there!'

'Aw this is hilarious, yir missin' the show,' came the screaming reply.

Mercifully, there were no reports of any club members killed or maimed at the 'Gunfight At The Not-So-OK Corral.

The rather grandiose, magnificent and somewhat posh destination of the Tomdoun Hotel in Glen Garry, situated on the road to Kinloch Hourn, had oddly been chosen as a weekend base for seven members one fine summer, albeit to reside in a hired bunkhouse. Built in 1895 as a sporting lodge, the resplendent building played host mainly to a wealthy clientele of those wishing to shoot and fish on the surrounding lands of the vast estate. There was, however, a public bar, which meant peasants and commoners from the lower classes could spend their money and drink as freely as the lord or lady standing next to them.

The hour was getting on when the minibus pulled up outside the hotel and the well-oiled rabble stumbled off and into the busy bar to ask where the bunkhouse was. A well-spoken gentleman informed them that, unfortunately, the bunkhouse was already double-booked, but they had a 'lesser' residence round the back which he could offer at £2 a night. The group's faces lit up at this unexpected bargain.

'Follow me lads, and I'll show you to it.'

They grabbed their gear and were taken to a dimly lit area to the rear of the hotel, where the gentleman pointed to what looked like a dilapidated shack. 'Make yourselves comfy lads,' and with that, he was off back to the bar. They were stopped in their tracks, momentarily speechless as they hesitantly entered and the light revealed their abode for the weekend.

Joe broke the silence first as the rest stared in disbelief. 'This izna a bunkhoose, it's a complete an' utter SHITEHOOSE!'

There before them lay a 13 foot square box with no windows, benches around the walls and a pishy, manky old carpet layered with enough mouse shit to fill a lorry. An empty sleeping bag was already laid out in one corner.

Johnny V Diff piped up, 'Ach it canna be that bad, sumdeez aridee pyed thir twa quid fir the night.'

True, these boys were no strangers to hardship who embraced the rough and ready with a passion and indeed, a few of them had enjoyed the pleasure of dossing in a barn in Kintail with the cooz still in it, but this shithole was on a completely different level, and they were having to pay for the pleasure of sleeping in it! The initial shock soon mellowed as they returned to the bar, where they made sure enough drink was consumed that would guarantee a drunken coma to forget where they were sleeping. It was here, whilst enjoying the pleasantries, that they found out who actually had commandeered the real bunkhouse. A group of fishermen from Fife who, by all accounts, could drink like the fish they were trying to catch. One guy was seen holding onto the bar, totally unable to put a sentence together. Several times the barman asked what he wanted, but all the inebriated angler could get out was 'drink.'

'Yes,' replied the barman, who by now was beginning to lose his patience, 'we do have a fine selection of wines, ales and spirits, but can you be more specific with your choice?'

'Drink,' came the slurred reply once more. The barman had heard enough and moved to the other end of the bar to serve someone who could actually talk. The NCR boys were in complete awe at the Fifers' drunken performance unfolding before them. Alas, near midnight, it was time to head back to the cesspit for some kip as there were mountains to be bagged in the morning, and so they left the riotous rabble behind. The rogue sleeping bag in the corner remained empty for now. Joe had drawn the short straw and had to sleep on the floor amongst the mouse droppings as there was no space left on the benches. As the men lay in snoring slumber, the peace was shattered by a wailing scream. Joe had just been awoken by a mouse running over his face and was not too chuffed.

Calm eventually returned and all was well as the men got back to their sweet dreams, but this was only a temporary lull, as around 3.00am the door crashed open and in fell the owner of the mystery sleeping bag. It was one of the Fife anglers, and he was steaming drunk. The light went on and straight into his bag he crawled. Two short hours passed when mayhem erupted once more in the shed from hell. The door shuddered with loud banging as a fist rattled hard on it then opened and a voice called in 'Come on Tam, shake yir arse, it's time to go.'

On went the light once more and Tam, who could barely stand a few hours earlier, got to his feet and grabbed his sleeping bag. Someone called out, 'Wut the bloody hell's goin' on?'

'Wir goin' awa fishin', replied Tam.

Johnny shot back quick as a flash, 'Fir fuck sake, the fish wull stull be in thir beds, it's only 5 o' clock!' The door closed and Tam was gone.

As knackered as they were from the night's shenanigans, the day turned out to be one of near perfection with blazing sunshine, blue skies and hardly a drop of wind as they scaled the summits of Spidean Mialach and Gleadhraich then dropped all their height before a final assault on Sgùrr a' Mhaoraich. They were rewarded for their efforts with heavenly views all around and the inevitable game of naming the surrounding peaks went into overdrive.

The bar in the Tomdoun that night was a much quieter affair as the Fifers had left the building to the great relief of the barman who was glad to see the back of them. There were, however, a couple of ghillies in and a rather posh looking gentleman decked out in the tweed uniform who was scooping away on whisky while his wife sat looking extremely bored and his young son looking even more bored than his bored mother.

It wasn't long before the ghillies popped the question to the NCR boys and asked what they were up for. When 'the mountains' came the reply, the two ghillie friends had very differing views. One was adamant that 'Hillwalkers were a bloody pain in the arse, scaring deer away when he and his clients were trying to blast their heads off and generally, a nuisance being on the land and scarring it.' His friend jumped to the mountain men's defence and argued that the hillwalking fraternity brings much-needed revenue to many rural communities and doesn't cause any problems being out there.

Tweed Guy had been eavesdropping from the next table and soon chucked his tuppence worth in with a very gentry opinionated view that hillwalkers shouldn't be anywhere near the estate lands. This attitude infuriated the lads, and the mood was turning visibly sour. The two ghillie friends were nearly coming to blows with each other while Hooray Henry was in danger of having his teeth removed. And with that very Scottish trait of friendship for strangers and 'wir ah Jock Tamson's bairns' the threatening Wild West saloon brawl was averted. Soon, drams were being bought for each other, stories were swapped, laughter bellowed out, men patted their fellow men on the back and a roaring sing-song retold episodes of the Jacobite Uprising. Life is funny.

Tweed Guy had forgotten he was Tweed Guy and had dropped the 'gentry front' to enjoy some great banter and conversation with the common folk. He had also enjoyed about a barrel of malt whisky, and it was to everyone's horror when he said his cheerios to the company and staggered into his Range Rover to drive his utterly bored wife and soundly sleeping son home.

Further to the west of the Tomdoun Hotel, the road ends at the tiny settlement of Kinloch Hourn, where the arduous and challenging walk to Barrisdale bothy begins. This is a serious undertaking, especially when tackled in the wee small hours of darkness following a session in the pub and a pack weighing a ton on the back. In sections, the narrow track is no place for a trip, as a fall down the embankment could possibly lead to a battle for survival in the deep blackness of Loch Hourn. None of this is made any easier when some of the more devious club members have thought it hilarious to forge ahead, turn off their head torches, then jump out of the fern bushes and scream at the first unsuspecting victim who has nearly died on the spot with fright.

During one of these many visits to Knoydart, a group had descended from the multi-ridged summit of mighty Ladhar Bheinn and were wearily approaching the bothy after a long day when they were stopped dead in their tracks. A man was lying slumped motionless over the steering wheel of an old tractor. Fearing the worst and panicking as to how to alert the authorities (in these pre-mobile phone days) in such a remote location, it wasn't until the Bonnie Prince approached to inspect the body.

'Is he dade?' asked someone nervously.

With a wee shoogle, the 'dade man' stirred into life.

The Bonnie Prince was able to comfort the group and replied, 'Nah, he's no' dade. He's absolutely pished!' The response was that of loud cheers and howls of laughter as the men helped the inebriated estate worker on his merry way back to his cottage.

There must surely have been something in the water in these parts where it concerned ghillies and estate workers, as one particularly boisterous bothy night, one of these very characters from a nearby cottage was passing and had heard the sing-song raging, so decided to pop his head in.

'Come away in an' gie wiz a sang,' he was invited. Sure enough, ten minutes later, he was back with a bottle of malt and joined the thick of the action. It is told by those who were still up and witnessed it that his fuming wife burst through the door at 5.00am and extricated her buckled husband to face her fiery wrath.

The final wee tale involved a certain character named 'Campbell' who used to maintain the estate and check in on the bothy from time to time. For those who remember him, he had a distinct glass eye, and some would say a rather unfriendly manner. The NCR boys had spent another successful weekend climbing the many surrounding summits and celebrated late into the night. As they tidied the bothy and readied for the long walk back to Kinloch Hourn the following morning, the man Campbell entered then barked, 'Have you lot put your donations into the box?' pointing to a locked metal container with a slot. Now there is no way of knowing if this was his own personal banky for his whisky kitty or if it really did go to help the estate, but grudgingly, some money was deposited, which seemed to lighten him up a little, and he began some idle chit-chat. Cliffy the Jacobite was brushing away at the dust on the floor and very innocently said to Campbell, 'Ach yull no' hae much tae dae in these parts, do ya?'

He'd been as well accusing Campbell solely for the Massacre of the MacDonalds at Glencoe.

With steam bellowing from his ears and foam gathering round his mouth, Campbell seethed, 'Not have much to do? You impudent clown. If you have a look out the door, you'll see there's thousands of acres which I have to tend to!' That was the point when the stampede raced for the door. It was time to leave.

Peg Leg Meets the Plegosaurus

Captain Peter stood at the helm, an' cast a wicked eye
Wiz it Long John Silver me boys? Or the ghost o' Captain Bligh?
They say it wiz the former, fir they baith hud gammy legs
While the cut-throat band afore him sang, hymns fae a powder keg
Ten buccaneers o' mayhem – an' a skull an' crossbones flag
Headin' fir bonnie Dundonnell, an' a feast o' hills tae bag
Shenavall bothy guest hoose, nae finer sight yull see
Wi' a guardian called An Teallach, collectin' ah yir entry fees

Now jist afore we start, Peter's handicap ehl divulge
A cartilage op on a busted knee, an' a massive bandage bulge
Twa weeks only hud passed, but the lure o' the hills wiz strong
King Kong couldna hud him back, twa weeks wiz far too long
'Hey Peg Leg howz it goin?' 'A wee bit sair but fine,'
The galleon's sails unfurled, an' the ship sailed north A9
Wid the wee man mak it through, the sufferin' an' the pain?
Or wiz an airlift on the cairds, an' eez efforts ah in vain?

The forced march inta the bothy, passed aff withoot inci-dent
An' the perty waited patiently, fir twa faces that they kent
Big Betty an' Jimmy D, hud left port wi' Dougie Mac
Three stouts in the Aultguish boozer, then the squad wir back on track
But Dougie soon perted company, fir a weekend chillin' oot
While Jimmy D an' Big Betty sauntered, doon the wrang bliddee route
They missed the critical turn aff, fir Paradiso Shenavall
An' hit the hovel o' Achneigie, whar pal blamed angry pal

The tranquil strath now thundered, wi' expletive overload
As dumb an' dumber searched the dark, fir the Pimpernel abode
Twa lambs in a highland hell-hole, seekin' the shepherd Peter
But twa stray lambs in Peg Leg's flock, widna tak him fae eez beer
Nah he wiz far too busy, swallyin' like a hungry pig
A drunken swine in a napalm rumpus, an' a one-legged bothy jig
Eventually the door unlatched, an' the hapless twa came in
The cat hud dragged them through the heather, an' shredded half thir skin

THE GHILLIES

A brilliant July mornin' - wiz blessed wi' a pale blue sky
An' the rollin' braes o' the Fisherfield Six, caught every bagger's eye
Peg Leg eyed them jealously, then said, 'ehl mibbee jist dae one'
'Beinn a' Chlaidheimh, then ehm aff, tae soak some summer sun'
The Abhainn Strath na Sealga, allowed them through her jaws
Thank Christ it wuzna springtime, when the season's snowfall thaws
Now fir some serious marchin', on a heather treadmill hike
A hike that by 7.00pm, puir tattered feet widna like

They reached thir first objective, wi' Peg Leg goin' well
Fightin' hard through ache an' pain, but the knee wiz startin' tae swell
Next stop, the peak Sgùrr Ban, then a push on summit three
An' tae thir horror Peg Leg followed, on a masochistic spree
'Ach yir only young an' daft once,' said the 30-something chap'
'Fit tae drink an' fit tae jig – sure, fit tae bliddee drap
An' so the day continued, wi' A' Mhaighdean the jewel in the croon
Then one last pull up Ruadh-Stac Mòr, afore they ah headed doon

Wi' a sheer monumental effort, Peg Leg hud bagged the lot
Then the perty came across a beast, fae *The Land That Time Forgot*
A remnant o' the ancient forest, that looked like a dinosaur
They ca'd it 'Plegosaurus' – Big Flatters corrected 'Plesiosaur'
'Wir no' carin' wut the hell it's ca'd, it's goin' on the fire!'
An extinct lump o' pine or oak, fir a dino funeral pyre
Big Geordie an' Betty heaved it, ower twa rivers an' the Strath
A kerry o' epic proportions, but the pair hud some guid laughs

The anti-Pharisee hullabaloo, got aff tae a flyin' start
Whar rules an' laws went oot the windee – shipped aff in a cart
Warlocks drank like dromedaris, fae Shenavall's oasis pool
An' each man did eez best tae prove, that HE wiz the bigger fool
But Jimmy D jist sat there, like a moose in a lion's den
'Here lads, tak ma half bottle, eh canna match you liquor-trained men'
The natives did a war-dance, an' worshipped whisky gods
An' toasted men o' the sober ilk, wha's breed deserved applause

The fire wiz runnin' low an' so, the Plegosaurus got dragged in
A sacrifice in a bed o' embers, aff tae heaven tae join eez kin
Now, Big Betty wiz feelin' the pace, a pace that forced some tae bed
A decision they wid soon regret, when Betty brought chaos an' dread
He picked up the Plegosaurus, an' burst inta slumberland
Dense smoke filled the room sae thick, 'BETTY YIR OOT o' HAND!'
Wi eez pet back in the fire, he cackled the laugh o' a crone
But the numpty totally forgot, that choked room wiz his OWN!

A Sunday mornin' nightmare, an' a breakfast hangover as well
'Right, wha's up fir An Teallach, an' the ridge fear citadel?'
Maist o' the troops fell inta rank, while a few used 'rubber ear'
'Hingin' aff they bliddee pinnacles? Yir right, we CANNA HEAR!'
They packed an' left the safties, an' waved a cheery goodbye
As Mac surfaced at a skylight, wi' the look o' a man goin' tae die
'Hey Mac, are ya goin' fir a summit?' But eez answer they already knew
A language as blue as the skyline, kicked aff wi' an F an' a U

Wi' full packs they toiled an' puffed, tae the foot o' the scary arete
The sound o' crashin' bottles echoed, an' fear turned hope tae regret
Like Hannibal's elephant army, they stuck tae mountain track
As Big Geordie an' Johnny went direct, an' filled thir breeks wi' cac
An' wha' wiz up there perched, on the point o' Lord Berkeley's Seat?
That indomitable warrior Peg Leg, lookin' doon Toll an Lochain street
A total o' eight Munros digested, an' a knee full o' TNT
Four months later at the surgeon's door, 'Well Doc, it wiz like this ya see…'

'Peg Leg Meets the Plegosaurus' tells the story of Peter, a club regular whose knees had taken a bit of a battering over the years in pursuit of his love for football, cycling, keep-fit and of course, the mountains.

Finally, he could take the excruciating pain no more, which had been building and grinding and one of the knees was operated on to remove cartilage. Following this, the doctor provided some sound advice and told his patient to rest it for a generous period of time before gently easing the mobility back.

'Peg Leg' followed the professional man's words to the letter and gave the tender knee a grand total of a couple of weeks' rest. There was no way in hell he was missing a first club trip to Shenavall bothy and the chance to bag eight Munros (now only seven as the Fisherfield Six 'lost' one). And so it was, he embarked on a journey through pain and hell, marching miles, river crossings, thousands of feet climbing, jigging and hangover and achieved the unthinkable to add those ticks to the list.

Inevitably, the knee took a sound thrashing and a few months later, he crawled back in for another operation. The doctor may or may not have heard the 'real' story as to why Peg Leg had returned so soon.

CHAPTER 8

The Dangerous Brothers

A rough night

RONNIE MAC AND Big Geordie were two of the characters who had emerged from that wild and wonderful group of members who had given the club a new lease of life in the 1980s. Ronnie had served his mountain apprenticeship from a young age, going out walking and climbing with his father, while Geordie was a relative newcomer to outdoor life.

Both had grown up in the rough Dundee housing scheme of Fintry during a period when the youth gangs were rife in the city and the chance of a proper tear-up or getting your head kicked in was never far away, especially if caught in the wrong place at the wrong time. With danger lurking just over the roads of rival schemes and their various gangs, Big Geordie, along with many of his mates, had joined the Fintry Shams in order to protect their turf and sometimes, 'invade' that of their enemies. The passing of time thankfully left the youthful years of aggro and scrapping behind, and they went on to form a solid friendship and nurture a great love of the mountains which endures to this day.

Full attention and energy were now focused on the Munros and any other summits which took their fancy. It became apparent very quickly that the duo had little or no fear of tackling dangerous routes, or more accurately, routes that were not recognised as normal and safe hillwalking routes. They earned the nickname 'The Dangerous Brothers' after the stage and TV act of the wacky and mental alternative comedy duo of Ade Edmondson and the late Rik Mayall. Crazy escapades were witnessed first-hand by others or retold by the pair themselves and played down in an almost casual manner.

On scaling the summit of Devil's Point in the Cairngorms, they decided that the quickest way down to Corrour bothy was to literally drop off the front and pick their way directly down the insanely steep and craggy face to the Lairig Ghru floor. On a similar occasion, after bagging the Munro trio of Beinn Liath Mhòr, An Sgùrr Ruadh and Maol Chean-dearg, a small group was gathered on the latter summit in a howling gale when Big Betty enquired as to what descent they could safely take to get back to Torridon. Careful study of the map and visuals dictated that north and north-east were out of the question.

Ronnie Mac had other plans and coolly replied, 'Ach, wull jist drap right aff the front direct. It looks a piece o' pish.' North-east it was, with a terrified comrade clinging on to clumps of grass, rock and anything else that would hold his weight to save him from plunging down the mountain, while the Dangerous Brothers descended like they were on a Sunday stroll.

On a winter outing to the Beinn a' Ghlò group in Highland Perthshire, the pair were involved in an epic battle with the elements as gusts of wind hit 90 to 100 miles per hour, lashing the mountains with an unforgiving ferocity. They had both elected to leave behind their crampons, which was a huge mistake. Incredibly, they somehow managed to scale Càrn Liath and Bràigh Coire Chruinn-bhalgain, then, refusing to give in, they set their sights on the final peak of Carn nan Gabhar.

As they dropped to the bealach then ascended the final ridge, they were exposed to savage westerly gusts which began to increase to ever more dangerous levels. Without crampons, they were swept off their feet and blown across the icy surface with ease. The only thing saving them was hitting the deck as each gusting roar approached, then hammering the ice-axes in as anchors. As soon as it passed, it was up and go again. With only a hundred yards or so to the summit, the Brothers had to admit defeat and accept they were no match for the power of Mother Nature. In true style, the duo adopted their tried and tested plan of 'ach, wull jist head doon here' and made their escape to the east, out of the gales but onto treacherously steep and icy snow slopes.

It wasn't until they had safely descended that Big Geordie realised his friend was struggling and wanting to sit down and sleep. Ronnie was in the clutches of early hypothermia as frequent snow showers combined with rain lower down had mercilessly soaked through their inadequate clothing. It was imperative that they both kept moving and tried to generate some warmth. During a river crossing which was raging and in spate, Ronnie chucked his ice-axe over, but it never reached the other bank and was washed away. Frozen, drookit and thoroughly bedraggled, the pair finally arrived at their car near Loch Moraig and quickly changed into dry clothes. This moment had Geordie crying with laughter as Ronnie removed his old saturated ex-army hooded jacket, which had some weird charcoal lining and left his body a black manky mess. The heating was set to full blast and a kettle boiled up for some hot soup as they reflected on another crazy adventure.

Big Davie was a larger-than-life character who worked in the NCR stores department and would often mock the Dangerous Brothers in passing, questioning their masculinity and brutally teasing them on their mountaineering hobby. 'Whar is it this weekend ya couple o' pussies? Awa shaggin' sheep in yir tent? Twa o' yiz zipped into one sleepin' bag?'

Eventually, they'd had enough and threw down the gauntlet to the big man. 'Ok motormouth, come up the mountains wi' us an' wull see whaz pussies.' With an audience around him on the shop floor, he couldn't decline and so accepted the offer. Now, Davie was called 'big' for a reason. He had a huge barrel chest, a non-existent neck, hands like the paws of a grizzly bear and a pair of thighs like tree trunks, and he liked nothing better than going to the local gym and pulverising the heavy punchbag. He convinced himself this hillwalking malarkey would be a stroll in the park, and he would leave the two 'pussies' trailing in his wake.

The Dangerous Brothers chose Glencoe and the magnificent Buachaille Etive Mòr to blood their novice mountaineering friend who had continued the insults and the taunts all the way up in the car. The lads had supplied Davie with a pack and some gear, but on his feet, he wore a pair of battered old steel-toe-capped work boots. The route was not the standard tourist path up the Coire na Tulaich, for that would have been far too easy. Oh no, they wanted Big Davie to have a day he would not forget in a hurry. No page had been turned in any guidebook for assistance or reference. They had a rough idea where Crowberry Gully lay and so it was, the horns were locked, and battle was about to commence. With no sign of either a rope or any jangly bits, Big Davie should have backed down right there and then, conceded defeat and taken the lads to a nearby bar for a pint.

The trio crossed the moor with the mass of the Buachaille standing daunting and menacingly before them. An early morning blanket of cloud and mist dominated the upper half of the mountain.

'Wuts the plan?' asked Davie. 'An' whars the path?'

'Jist keep climbin' tull we canna climb any further then yull ken wir at the tap,' answered Ronnie.

It is worth mentioning at this point that the climbing of Crowberry Gully is a serious undertaking and requires a good degree of skill and competency on rock, especially on the steeper sections. In winter, it is regarded as one of the Scottish classics. Davie was about to enter a mountaineering baptism of fire. Initially, he coped well enough in the circumstances, but the higher they went, a deep wave of self-doubt began to engulf him. Even though he was in the company of two friends, supporting and encouraging his every move, he felt very alone and exposed in the dark and scary enclosure. It didn't help his confidence either when they came across a dead sheep and Davie asked the lads how the hell it had managed to get up here?

Geordie's answer was unnerving and to the point. 'Ach, that's fell fae up there, poor beast.'

They reached a chockstone which barred their progress and had to be overcome with some difficulty. Ronnie climbed up ahead and pulled, while Geordie was left with the undignified job of pushing the big man up by his arse. With the cloud rapidly lifting, Davie began to freak out as he looked back in horror to see where he actually was. He was way out of his depth and decided he was going no further up the gully. The Brothers had a quick discussion and devised a new plan, which involved Geordie leading the way up the vertically challenging rock wall to the right. This, in turn, led them on to the huge mass of Central Buttress.

Over time, the memory of the fine detail as to the exact route they took has evaporated like the swirling cloud, but some highly charged incidents were never to be forgotten. As the terrain became ever more perilous and demanding, the pair were mindful of keeping their friend in complete safety while finding a route that would take them to the summit. The job of having Big Davie shit his breeks in total fear had long been achieved, but the breeks were about to have a deluge of shit that was unsurpassed in the history of one shitting their breeks.

Geordie was leading the way across a ledge that was sensationally exposed with a massive drop below when Davie, following in the middle, stopped and shouted out, 'That's it, ehm no' movin', ehv hud enough!' No amount of persuasion or reassurance was going to get him mobile. He was cragfast (stuck on the rock) and overcome with paralysing fear. The situation was truly critical. It is worth remembering that these were pre-mobile phone days, so a simple call to the Mountain Rescue Team was out of the question and in any case, these boys were made of sterner stuff with a mindset of 'get in a mess, assess, then deal with it'.

Geordie had climbed onto another ledge above, but there was no way he could pull the mass of Davie's bulk up by himself. Ronnie was going to have to go completely out of balance and hold onto Davie's clothes, then climb around him and hope that they wouldn't both plunge to their deaths. In fact, there was a real danger that all three could have departed together as Davie had one hand grasping desperately onto Geordie's boot while Ronnie made the suicidal manoeuvre. (Ronnie would later admit that it was one of the few moments during all his years in the mountains where he felt his life may end. Big Davie, on the other hand, would later admit that he felt his life would end every 30 seconds that day.) The situation was almost Charlie Chaplin-like for sheer comedy value, had it not been set in such a grim and dangerous theatre.

Ronnie thanked the gods of Buachaille Etive Mòr for sparing their lives, then was able to join Geordie and pull their big comrade up to join them on their narrow stance. Just as Davie tried to pull himself together, he was nearly forced over the edge in disbelief as Geordie calmly announced, 'That this was as good a place as any to have a wee piecey break.'

'Wut, HERE?' Davie asked, completely flabbergasted. 'You twa are seriously aff yir fuckin' rockers!'

The three of them were sat perched like eagles on a clifftop eyrie. While his friends delved into their sandwiches and flasks and shared some light banter, Davie remained silent and motionless with his fingers welded onto the hillside.

'Are ya no' hungry?' asked Ronnie.

No reply was needed as thoughts of murder raced through his fear-swamped mind. If he could just get over to them and strangle them. The familiar whirr from a helicopter's rotor blades broke a brief lull in the conversation with Geordie's keen eyes first to spot it.

'Eh canna see it,' said Davie as his eyes scanned the sky for the metal bird.

'No' up there ya daftie. There it is doon in the glen.' Geordie's words brought horror and anxiety right back to the big man as he realised he was higher than something that flew in the sky. How they ever managed to get their completely inexperienced friend to the summit is anybody's guess, but they did. Back in the old climber's bar at the Kingshouse, Big Davie sat gripping a pint with a few empties scattered in front of him. The first two didn't stand a chance and hadn't touched the sides. Now totally relaxed, the worn-out work boots discarded for his favourite slippers, he looked both the Dangerous Brothers in the eye, then said, 'You twa are seriously mentul an' eh canna believe ehm stull alive an' able to enjoy a pint.'

As they laughed heartily, they found it pertinent to withhold any admission that Davie might just be spot on with his observations and that they too had been out on a limb on more than one occasion. They afforded him not an inch.

So, did the big man learn a lesson from his crag-clinging episode in Glencoe? Did he hell. Within a matter of days, his voice could be heard booming across the factory, once again ripping into the Dangerous Brothers and telling his audience how the mountain men had failed to break him.

And hindsight is a wonderful thing, they say, but no human being has ever possessed the skills to unlock the secrets of. Ronnie and Geordie bided their time before throwing down a second gauntlet, which ultimately would prove decisive in finally gaining Big Davie's respect, not just for themselves but for the at times rugged and testing hardship of the mountain environment. This time, they upped the ante and took him to Glen Doll in winter, where they dragged him over the partly frozen waterfall at the head of Corrie Fee, then later, onto a series of highly exposed ledges on Craig Rennet. There was no mercy shown this time, not even for the fact that Davie's toes were getting near-frostbitten in his trusty, battered old steel-toe-capped work boots.

Amid the hustle and bustle of the climber's bar in the Glen Clova Hotel, a large-framed character sat nursing a pint beside the fire. He turned to his two friends and said with a large hint of deja vu, 'You twa are completely mentul,' but this time he added, 'an' eh am NEVER comin' back oot wi' you maniacs EVER again!' And he never did.

Club Founder, Frank Anderson climbing in Glen Clova, 1950s.

May 1959, members enjoying a wee biley-up in Glenshee.

October 1958, a challenging crossing of the River Doll, Glen Clova.

Davie Foote on a river crossing, 1960s.

Members resting in Glen Clova, May 1955.

Dundee and proud.

Jimmy Carson (left) and Davie Foote (right) were part of the club's Rescue Team.

A favourite wild campsite in Glen Shiel during the '70s and '80s, much to the annoyance of the official campsite.

Camping at Inveroran, 1970s.

Blackburn of Pattack, a favourite bothy with the club now sadly long gone – it burned down in the 1990s.

Ronnie Mac, one half of the Dangerous Brothers, descending the face of Devil's Point, 1980s.

Big Geordie, the other half of the fearless Dangerous Brothers, on the face of Devil's Point, 1980s.

A well-earned beer on some far-flung summit, 1980s.
L–R: the Bonnie Prince, Fred Mac (sitting), Phil, Cliffy the Jacobite.

A parched crew having just done a huge weekend in the hills, arrive at Kingshouse Hotel only to find the bar closed, 1980s.

Piecey break at Ba Bridge near Inveroran during the 1980s.

Lunch at the Upper Lunch Hut near the Spittal of Glenshee, 1980s.

L–R, Big Geordie, Neil, Geordie F and Ronnie Mac in Glencoe, 1980s.

Johnny V Diff on Ben Vrackie, late 1980s.

V Diff and one of the many buses used for weekenders, at Kinloch Rannoch Outdoor Centre, late 1980s.

Bothy culture in Ruigh Aiteachain, November 1991. The legendary Big Flatters on the right.

Winter Meet to Ruigh Aiteachain Bothy, 1991.

The character Dougie Mac and some of the group before the infamous 'Dougie Mac tour' of Pinnacle Ridge on Skye, June 1992. L–R: Dougie Mac, BB, John B, Tardy, 'Crack o' Dawn' Colin (sitting).

Piecey break on Sgòr na h-Ulaidh, Glencoe, 1990s.

Mikey Fitz and Brucie climbing on Arran, 1990s.

Big Geordie and Johnny V Diff on the Corrag Bhuidhe pinnacles of An Teallach, 1990s.

Flying the flag on A' Mhaighdean on the weekend when Peg Leg managed all eight Munros, 1990s.

One of many trips to Shenavall bothy in the 1990s.
L–R: Cammy, Tardy, BB, Farfir, Joe T, Sweary Doug.

Winter camping at Auchallater near Braemar, 1990s.

Summit party on Slioch, September 1996 – and the end of Cammy's Munro conquest… well, until he did his second round.

Johnny V Diff crossing the super exposed 'drawbridge' on Liathach, September 1996.

Club member abseiling off the In Pinn, Skye during the 1990s.

A few tunes on Am Basteir, Skye, June 1998. Shortly afterwards, Dougie Mac fell off the face and was nearly killed.

With the legendary Martyn Bennett in Skye before the night of mayhem, June 1999.

Full squad enjoying a wee swally during a long May Day weekend at Glengarrisdale bothy on the Isle of Jura, early 2000s.

Gorton bothy, Jan 2024. Cal, V Diff and Mark enjoying the 'bothy TV'.

Carn Dearg Hut, Glen Doll, Xmas Meet. Celebrating 75 years of NCR Hillwalking & Climbing Club, December 2024.

CHAPTER 9

Carry on Camping (Part 2)

Wahrz the toilet?

IN SCENES WHICH could have come straight out of the hilarious *Carry On Camping* film, we return for another helping of canvas catastrophes spent under the stars. The need for safety in the confines of a tent is of paramount importance, but sometimes things go out of our control, be it a turn for the worse in the weather or just a plain old accident. And then, of course, there are the times when alcohol may have played a part in the gross stupidity which followed.

Camping out in winter is not for the faint-hearted, and dealing with extreme temperatures is not everyone's cup of tea. It takes a hardy character to ignore the discomfort of freezing weather where just getting a sleep can be nigh on impossible. This was especially true in the days when a cosy sleeping bag was an expensive luxury and most of the group had bags that were about as insulated as a quilted crisp packet. The most effective way to combat this was to put on as many clothes as possible, but even this method would sometimes struggle inside the sub-zero cocoon. The old wafer-thin sponge mats offered very little warmth either.

There was, however, an alternative which involved some assistance from one of man's oldest friends – fire. The club had pitched up once more in an old favourite spot at Kintail and the group had enjoyed a huge winter's day on the hill, followed by the full session in the local bar. It was a rather tipsy crew who staggered back to the tents, their breaths like puffs of smoke in the bitterly cold air as they talked nonsense, sang, cursed and laughed before crawling into their arctic abodes for the night. Davie San complained to himself that his feet were like the proverbial 'blocks of ice' and the problem needed a remedy. His plan involved firing up the gas stove, squirming into his sleeping bag, then holding his feet above the flame, thus bringing some very welcome warmth.

He was probably already sleeping before the angels had got to the end of the chorus 'Get the fire brigade' from The Move's 1968 classic song 'Fire Brigade'. Thankfully and rather miraculously, the next sentence does not include the words inferno and death. He awoke (God only knows how) to the strong and pungent smell of burning material and cooking flesh. Then the screaming started. Bruce rushed to his friend's aid and was horrified to find Davie with some serious burns. His back was one huge blister, but his main concern was how to explain this to his wife without mentioning alcohol. The drive back to Ninewells Hospital in Dundee was one of incredible agony. It seems the flame had somehow been smothered, or the gas had run out, leaving the bag and mat to smoulder away, but either way, he was one very lucky camper. The tent had taken a hit too and was left with a big hole in the groundsheet. *(This hole was to feature a few months later when Davie had recovered and was back out camping with the club on a meet to Tyndrum. The weather had been hellish with a combination of snow, sleet and heavy rain hammering the gathering, so much so that a small stream had formed and was running straight under Davie's tent. The hole provided the perfect release to form a spouting geyser and quickly drench all contents inside, forcing him to relocate to a railway bothy.)*

CARRY ON CAMPING (PART 2)

It was a similar set of circumstances which saw Bruce fall victim to the idea of installing a heating system in his tent on a winter meet. Cruachan on the north side of Loch Awe was the intended destination, but, as had happened many times in the past, the minibus pulled in at the Luib Hotel before Crianlarich for a few light refreshments, which predictably evolved into a night of riotous carnage. The owners always seemed to be one step ahead and let a few pints sink in before throwing in the kind offer of 'free camping' around the back. The thirsty mountaineers were easily lured with the liquid bait.

Along with the rest of the drunken rabble, Bruce and Farfar Tam were steaming when they left the bar and unzipped the tent flaps. A ravenous hunger now took over the pair, so the stove was fired up and a fry-up was hastily organised. With full and contented bellies, the decision was made to leave the stove on for a 'wee while longer' and cosy the place up while they had a 'wee lie doon'. Well, the inevitable happened, and eyelids which felt as heavy as a pair of dumbbells were soon tightly shut, and the tent rafters shook with the rumble of heavy snoring. At some point during the night, Bruce had stirred in his dream and thought that the heat had become almost 'real' feeling. His nose twitched and sensed the smell of burning feathers.

'Aw shite! Tam, uhm on fire!' he yelled, but Tam was too busy counting bridies and dreaming of fair maidens roaming around the sweet smelling berry fields of Forfar.

Lady Luck had favoured the pair of numpties and decided not to cremate them. She let Bruce off with a cooked leg and the need for a new sleeping bag.

A forecast for very heavy snow and blizzard conditions had not discouraged the adventurous band in the slightest as the minibus snaked its way up through Glenshee. The chosen site for the rough camp was just off the A93 road, south of Braemar at Auchallater, (which is now a car park). Spirits were lifted earlier, along with the liquid variety in the Spittal Hotel and the group were very grateful on reaching the site that the ground was still soft enough under the snow to insert tent pegs. Saturday dawned with a barrage of large snowflakes falling rhythmically and relentlessly, each one dancing its own path down from the heavily laden clouds. Small groups set off into the white hell, hopeful of achieving their various objectives.

Big Geordie and Big Betty had set their sights on the summit of An Socach, which they had made in good time, given that the snow was getting deeper by the hour. While descending in a white-out, they were both focused intensely on following a compass bearing into the nothingness and walked straight over a rocky outcrop. They had only fallen some 20 ft into deep, powdery snow and were extremely relieved that it wasn't a huge cliff. Although they found it hilarious that they had both plunged headfirst on the same step, it was a sharp reminder of the need to have accurate navigation in such difficult conditions.

Everyone had returned safely and shared their day's stories while firing up the stoves and cooking the tea before the forced march along to Braemar and what would be the welcoming bar in The Fife Arms. It was at this point that the group had a visit from the local constabulary, who were a 'little concerned' for the well-being of everyone and informed them that they were about to close the snow gates, which would effectively mean that the campers would be cut off and isolated. The Boys In Blue warned that even more snow was on the way overnight.

Johnny V Diff put their minds at ease and called back, 'Ach dinna worry aboot us officers, we're awa to hit the boozer an' git pished. We'll be just fine here.'

The coppers laughed and shook their heads in disbelief at these Dundonian crackpots, then left and were on their merry way. Thoughts of being stranded for a day or two or more never entered the equation at any point. It was just over two miles to the pub, but this lot were in the mood and thirsty and covered the snow-packed road in good style. Would the return journey be the same? It most certainly would not.

Friend held up friend as the snaking, zigzagging pished-up procession valiantly attempted to follow their own head torch beams back to the campsite. They were very grateful that the second blizzard had not yet materialised, and it was one sorry, broken bunch who fell back into camp. Tent walls were banked up with snow and welcomed each man inside their frigid retreats.

CARRY ON CAMPING (PART 2)

While some gorged on crisps and peanuts, others went straight to slumberland to kickstart the snoring orchestra. Big Betty decided to fire up his stove for a 'few minutes' and heat the place up. Around eight in the morning, he awoke to a gentle and melodic purring sound. The two-man Vango felt strangely warm for the time of year. If truth be told, it was bloody toasting. He opened his eyes and there, only six inches from his head, stood his stove joyfully still burning away with a very small flame. His saving grace had been the fact that he was so inebriated he had lain unconscious and motionless the whole night. The second storm never came, the snow gates reopened, and they all lived happily ever after... well, for a wee while.

The little village of Cannich lies some 12 miles to the west of Drumnadrochit in Inverness shire and provides an excellent starting point for access further west to a goldmine of mountains in Glen Affric and those to the north of Loch Mullardoch. A healthy party of 13 had attended with the promise of a favourable and sunny weekend forecast, and they were not disappointed as two separate parties swarmed over the summits to the north as far as An Socach and down to Màm Sabhail in the south. It was some very tired and fatigued bodies that returned to camp, but everyone was also elated at accomplishing their planned circuits.

A glorious sunshine still beamed in the early evening as the familiar hum of stoves and clanking of bivvy tins cut through the tranquil scene. Big Geordie was taking in the whole setting, tent flaps open, tea cooking away on the old Primus stove and a tin of beer going down like golden nectar. The tatties and mince, however, were taking a lot longer than expected, and he knew the gas was running low so thinking it was empty, unscrewed the cannister, replaced it with a new one and was back in business. Unbeknown to the big man, the discarded canister was not empty, and the gas began to leak out in the porch. Suddenly, there was a big flash, and a fireball flew over his head, singeing his hair, eyebrows and tasher. The front of the tent was ablaze, so he quickly retreated to the rear, desperately thrashing at the flames with anything he could lay his hands on while screaming 'FIRE! FIRE! HELP!'

First on the scene was Mikey Fitz's girlfriend, who launched a pint of milk into the tent. This had absolutely no effect whatsoever in dousing the flames and Geordie would later joke that all it had achieved was to make him stink. They did eventually manage to extinguish the blaze, which left the tent looking like a burnt out wagon from an old Western cowboy movie. The session in the local bar that night was extra boisterous as the gang celebrated their singed comrade still being alive. Thankfully, no one put their foot in it and raised their glass, then uttered the words 'Ehl toast ya Geordie' as this would have been deemed as highly inappropriate.

Without a word of a lie or any attempt to sensationalise this unfortunate episode, the big man returned to the charred ruin that night and slept like a baby, while a myriad of stars twinkled brightly through the large and tattered holes.

One of the coldest camps the club was ever involved in happened during a January trip to the little village of Arrochar and a planned assault on bagging the mountains known affectionately as the 'Arrochar Alps'. Situated at the head of Loch Long, it is set in a stunningly picturesque area where rugged summits and lonely lochs abound. The problem for the group travelling was that none of them had ever camped in this particular area before. With the hour late, finding somewhere to rough camp in the dark was proving to be a big problem.

Reluctantly, the minibus pulled into the official campsite with many disgruntled voices protesting the thought of having to part with valuable drinking money and pay a couple of pounds to stay in their own tent. The air was filled with mutiny. They need not have worried, however, for the site owner, on hearing the commotion of bodies outside his house, came out raging and told them in no uncertain terms that 'the site was bloody closed for the winter.' He was dutifully supported by an equally raging Alsatian who looked like he wanted to eat hillwalkers. When someone threatened to set about it with an ice-axe, it was time to retreat and find another spot.

It was some time before a piece of 'camping paradise' was found, complete with well-maintained grass and a river nearby, but more importantly, the pubs were within walking distance. It never occurred to any of them that this ground may be too good to be true. The night was not unduly cold, sitting somewhere around freezing level with any snow confined to the mountain tops. Morning dawned as one of those perfect winter scenes, sun rising to blaze through a deep blue sky and not a drop of wind.

The realisation that they were camped on some kind of picnic area became very apparent but the wee hooses were up now and they were staying up. Some men were down to wearing just t-shirts as they hit the snowline of Beinn Narnain, that famed mountain whose caves could tell a million stories from the legendary characters holed up there from a bygone era. Beinn Ìme was taken in as well, whilst the small group who'd gone to Ben Vane had a day of epic, almost alpine proportions on the wonderfully steep and solid packed snow and ice.

When darkness fell in the early evening, the temperature dropped dramatically to bring an extremely bitter and savagely cold night, which the thermometer would later record a figure of -16C. The simple task of washing the pans and cooking utensils in the river almost had hardened mountain men crying for their mothers. The pub, as always, was lively and cosy, and the severe conditions were forgotten about for the time being. Concern had been growing earlier for two very experienced mountaineers within the club who had still not returned, and thoughts were now moving towards calling the Mountain Rescue.

Flatters and Pratchett had gone off to do their own thing that morning but really should have been back by now. No one suspected for a second that the pair of penny-watching, sobriety-supporting Englishmen would be scooping pints in another bar, but that's exactly what unfolded. The big question was how the hell they managed to jemmy open their padlocked wallets. It was agreed that they must have found a £20 note on the floor. When they finally appeared, rosy-cheeked, giggling and uncharacteristically half-canned, it was met with great relief to the others, who then informed them that they were on the verge of calling the Mountain Rescue. Flatters, in particular, who was as mountain tough as they came, was totally aghast and embarrassed at the mere thought of having a rescue team out looking for him, but his protests fell on deaf ears as the duo of apprentice bevvy merchants were soundly ripped by the pack.

With 'last orders' now a distant memory, they stotted back to the campsite where Dougie Mac and JB announced 'perty in oor tent lads.' The Vango which was equipped to sleep 'three', had ten bodies crammed in, producing a welcome warmth in contrast to the ultra-low temperature outside. A litre of whisky was offered up from Fergus, a newcomer to the club who hailed from the west coast and got the soiree off to a fine start with a rendition of 'Shoals o' Herring'. The gathering paid homage to this messiah, while the bottle instantly began doing the rounds. The fry-up fizzling away in the corner led a charmed life, balancing on the stove, but somehow survived the drunken melee.

It was late in the morning, as tents were being dismantled, when a stranger appeared and asked the group what the hell they were doing. A deeply hungover JB snapped back, 'Well, it's quite obvious pal, wir takkin wir tents doon.'

'This is a bloody Scout Camp, not a public campsite for any Tom, Dick or Harry to use,' he fumed.

'Well Scout's Honour, wiv nae Tom, Dick or Harry, here so thank you very much an' wull be seein' ya.'

The guy, who was a local warden, was left speechless as the mob hastily departed and waved goodbye to lovely Arrochar.

Water had played as much a part as fire did when it came to camping calamities, and a weekend visit to the beautiful island of Arran nearly brought a flooding disaster. The club had, in fact, first set foot on the island in the early 1980s. Back then, the Friday night ferry left too early in order to catch from Dundee so the delightful hostelries of Ardrossan would be hammered on a pub crawl, then guys would slither into their sleeping bags in the terminal and board the first crossing in the morning, something which would almost certainly never be allowed or tolerated nowadays.

Fast forward a decade, the club paid a long overdue return visit to the island in the hope of completing the Glen Rosa circuit. With a revised timetable now in operation, the Friday evening ferry was caught and bodies paced back and forth anxiously waiting for the shutters to open at the bar. Unfortunately, the rules stated that this couldn't happen until the ship had set sail. When it did, the NCR boys went into a frenzy buying double and treble rounds with the sole purpose of downing as many beverages as was humanly possible during the short crossing. Fifty-five minutes later, and with the ship about to dock at Brodick, the scene was one of sheer devastation with empties piled high on the tables. The large group was taxied up to the campsite in Glen Rosa, deposited at the top of a steep embankment and left to sort out their gear in the dark.

The following scenes can only be described as 'absolutely hilarious' when drunken individuals began descending to find a suitable spot to pitch their tents. Foul curses and screams rang out as men tripped and slipped, limbs flailing while tents and rucksacks took their own course. Campers who were already there must have thought the circus had arrived, and they wouldn't have been mistaken. Bodies arose in the morning to find a comical arrangement of scattered tents, with many pitched on the flat ground near the low, running river. Full breakfasts were soon being gorged in the hope of a quick cure for the hangovers when cries of 'help' began to ring out from the toilet block.

Wee Ecky had gone and locked himself in (as no one had obtained the security code) and could be seen through the metal grated gate with a very worried look on his face, the kind of look which thought he might rot and die in this prison latrine. He got no sympathy whatsoever as his so-called mates howled with laughter and let him stew for a bit before Big Betty went and rescued him, forcing his pal's jail door with a dessert spoon!

An assortment of routes were taken onto the nearby mountains while a couple of 'casualties' from the previous night's festivities opted for a long lie in camp. Bruce and Mikey Fitz were off an hour before the others and tackling climbing routes on Cìr Mhòr. The largest party took on the big challenge of the four Corbetts, starting at the subsidiary Top of Beinn Nuis, then onto Beinn Tarsuinn. As they traversed along the A' Chir Ridge, the weather took a turn for the worse and, although the cloud level stayed above the summits, a torrential downpour was unleashed, which was also charged with electrical current. *Poor Bruce and Mikey later reported that they were shitting themselves while positioned high on a rock face with streams of water running down the sleeves of their jackets and the metalwork on their climbing gear fizzling and crackling with static energy.*

The storm passed over for the time being and the summit of Cìr Mhòr was reached to reveal a full 360 degree stunning panorama of mountain ridges, glens and deep corries. Caisteal Abhail fell next before a return to Cìr Mhòr and a tricky descent (aided by a rope) to The Saddle between the final summit of Goatfell. It was here the heavens opened up, dropping a sustained and ferocious deluge of proper Scottish rain, much to the misery of the now drookit bunch who doggedly completed the circuit before hastily making their descent. Back at camp there was a hive of activity as those who had camped near the river were now frantically relocating to higher ground as the Glenrosa Water was in serious danger of bursting its banks.

The Gore-Tex clad platoon stepped back out into the monsoon arena with a forced march down into the bright lights of Brodick, seeking the first boisterous hostelry. A second monsoon came in the form of fine ales and spirits and the return journey called for a taxi job. Part Two of the 'Glen Rosa campsite Olympics' ensued as men involuntarily cartwheeled, back-flipped and face-planted once more down the steep embankment. (There was, of course, a track which was never located until departure.)

Bodies emerged from tents like extras from a zombie apocalypse film but instantly felt alive and human again when fellow zombie Joe, his tent surrounded by an array of multi-coloured Aftershock shot glasses, popped his head out to sheepishly announce that he had tried a 'wee fart' during the night. This had invariably gone wrong and led to a bag full of sludge. The glen erupted with the sound of uncontrollable laughter as campers fell about holding their sides.

Down at the quayside, the sun had put in a welcome appearance as the group enjoyed a wee meal from the chip shop while waiting on their ferry back to the mainland. Wee Ecky was still scoffing his sausage supper and enjoying the views when two unscrupulous, cunning characters crept up behind him and scattered a large bag of chips at his back. Five seconds later, the whole squadron of Arran's elite seagull bomber's swooped in, squawking and screeching like an airborne gang of possessed banshees. The forfeited bag of chips was worth every penny to witness Wee Ecky fleeing for his life, almost fearing that any delay might have seen him picked up and carried back to the clifftop hideout and devoured by the flock. No quarter was ever given or expected in return when it came to blatant childish behaviour.

There were many calamitous and chaotic camping episodes, too many to mention, but the penultimate disastrous instalment happened during a trip to the village of Crianlarich in Highland Perthshire. It was a full minibus which left Dundee on the Friday night with many members excited at the prospect of bagging a few Munros in and around the area. Someone knew of a spot for rough camping down by the River Fillan, so off they went, piling over a barbed wire fence weighed down with gear. As the tents were erected, getting water from the river proved to be problematic due to a drop of around 4 ft down the embankment. A cold and wintry downpour set in as the group made their way to the local Rod And Reel to quench any dry throats.

The first to arise the following morning were quickly made aware of the fact that the campsite had now become part of the River Fillan. Torrential rain had hammered all through the night, causing the river to rise significantly and burst its banks. A few 'lucky' campers had unknowingly pitched on little islands and were surrounded, while the not-so-lucky were saying good morning to some passing trout. JB, who had indulged most enthusiastically in last night's alco-festivities was spotted still sleeping soundly, his tent flaps open and the lower half of his sleeping bag submerged in the water. It was time to get the hell out of there.

Johnny V Diff had his plastic winter climbing boots on and assured himself his feet would stay bone dry as he dismantled his tent. Unfortunately for him, the wade to higher ground was knee-deep and filled his boots instantly. Pandemonium ensued all around as men feared they would be washed all the way down to Loch Tay. For the first (and only) time in the club's history, it was decided to abort the meet without a single glen being trodden or summit conquered. Worse was to follow, however, as the aged and rather clapped-out minibus refused to start. The call went out for all able-bodied men (which was everyone!) to put their shoulders to the rear and help get it started.

'Crack o' Dawn' Colin, who was well known for his liking of a wee 'hair o' the doag', was having none of such strenuous activities in the pishing rain and was spotted buggering off to the local shop for a large breakfast carry-out, much to the anger and protests of the disgruntled pushers and shovers. It was one sorry-looking, drookit and depressed band aboard a mobile heap of junk who finally limped back to Dundee. Well, apart from one steaming member tucked away in the corner, surrounded by a pile of empties, who enjoyed the journey immensely.

The final little story moves to more recent times and an era which has brought the hip and trendy idea of camping on vehicle roofs. For many members over the years, just getting into a tent on level ground has proved to be a massive challenge, especially following a full session in the pub and many tents have been flattened with poles bent beyond repair. The inventor of the rooftop tent was obviously a teetotaller and hadn't given any thought whatsoever to the campers who had purchased this great new product in good faith, but also liked to fall out of the pub at closing time. Johndo and Marko were about to give this new invention the proper factory test that it most certainly never had while in pre-production.

Following a huge day which took in the five Munros in and around Lochnagar, they returned to the van parked off the A93 road, then made straight for Braemar. They came to a halt behind the Invercauld Mews and debated whether to erect the tent there and then or have a few foaming ales first. As is nearly always the case, the little devils appeared on both men's shoulders and dragged them into the pub without any resistance being offered. The tent assembling was delayed... for a further six hours. Both men went out of the blocks rapidly and set about the fine ales and spirits on offer with wanton abandon. By midnight, any speech between the men was completely incomprehensible and strong legs that had carried them over mountain and moor earlier were now as stable as rubber stilts. Holding each other up, they staggered out into the night laughing like a pair of pished hyenas.

As they attempted to erect the tent, Johndo made the first critical error and forgot to release the Velcro straps, resulting in severe bending of the structure poles. After much cursing and giggling, they got the tent up a little and decided that would have to do and worry about it in the morning. Unfortunately, someone broke the ladder in half, which they thought was hilarious and with it now swinging about limply, the chance of climbing it was less than zero. Marko eventually helped hoist his inebriated mate onto the roof of the van, but he couldn't work out how to enter the ruin, so he opted to dive off and incorporate a commando roll into the movement. He landed like an anvil falling from the sky and instantly began moaning and groaning in agony. Marko was rolling about crying with laughter at his friend's failed Olympic stunt and was awarded a measly 2 out of 10 for the effort on the scorecard.

As the paralytic pantomime had neared its conclusion, the bar staff were seen locking up and making their way to their houses. God only knows what they had made of the two lunatics falling about the forecourt. Johndo (who miraculously hadn't broken any bones) decided to sleep IN the van and not ON it. Marko had brought his own tent with him and when the signs were blatantly clear that the rooftop battle was lost, he staggered off into the dark and pitched it on what he thought was a perfect spot. In the morning, he awoke, his body aching as he found himself spooning a large boulder with the other half of the tent on top of a small bush. It was maybe just as well they hadn't put the rooftop tent up before the pub. One can only imagine the results of having to get up for a pee during the night.

Thankfully, no club member or members (thus far) have progressed onto the extreme form of camping where the tent is pegged precariously into the side of a sheer cliff, hanging thousands of feet off the ground, although the stories following a full pish-up in the pub and trying to get inside would be interesting.

CHAPTER 10

Skye's the Limit

Essan bothy

FOR ANYONE REMOTELY interested in climbing mountains, completing the Munros or for those with a general love of beautiful scenery and landscape, there is nowhere else on the whole of the British Isles to match the majestic and encapsulating Island of Skye or *Eilean a' Cheò* (the Misty Isle) as it is often referred to in Gaelic. The jagged volcanic peaks of the Black Cuillin form the main focus for those wishing to challenge themselves and have done so for generations. Mainly formed from gabbro rock, they provide an excellent surface on which to grip, something which is extremely important whilst tackling the exposed narrow ridges and airy summits. Comprising of 12 Munros in total, the first sight of these daunting and imposing dark mountains for normal hillwalkers is enough to have some maybe reconsider their hobby options. They are most definitely not for the faint-hearted, where a good head for heights, steady feet and balance and good route-finding are essential. Occasionally, a rope, harness and some jangly bits can come in handy too. Attempting them with a raging hangover, or indeed pished, is certainly not recommended. This point was never explained to the club.

As was mentioned previously, a few club members from the early days had made the long trip to Skye to climb in the Cuillin, but it wasn't until the late 1980s that the club began an annual meet to the island, with most in search of the prized Munro summits. Those first couple of trips were a proper step into the unknown, with many not truly aware of what lay in wait for them. The alien landscape seemed almost lunar in appearance, such was the difference in geography from the rest of the country, and it was with an incredible naivety which saw a couple of members being labelled 'The Corrie Bashers' as they set huge rocks bouncing off down the cliffs, exploding in fragments as they went. This was innocently viewed as 'damn hilarious' until someone pointed out that these mountains were hugely popular with climbers and could be on any face at any given time, and who would certainly not appreciate a volley of humongous rocks raining down on them, however hilarious it may seem to the perpetrators.

Some had made the effort to indulge in a little reading and research of the various routes and names of the peaks, but it was to be a whole different ball game up on the ridge when looking at a scantily detailed map with an unreliable compass due to the magnetic pull in some of the rock. In the mist and rain, it was bordering on a suicide mission. Those club 'bagging pioneers' set off from Dundee aboard the old Yellow Submarine minibus with adventure in their hearts and ale in their bellies. The fact that that particular bus ever made it to the Kyle of Lochalsh was a miracle in itself. The hour was late when the ferry set sail for the short crossing over to Kyleakin and began the drive to find the fabled Cuillin mountains. It was at Sligachan that they came to a halt and attempted to locate a suitable spot to camp. The nearby official campsite was an absolute no-no as that would have cost valuable drinking tokens, so tents were erected on the ground near the hotel. Dougie Mac and JB, however, had taken it a little too far (or near as the case may be) and had set up the party tent on the lawn just outside some hotel windows. Picture the scene, with paying guests opening their curtains hoping to see magnificent Sgùrr nan Gillean in all its morning glory, but instead, being greeted by two dishevelled, bare-chested vagrants scratching their balls and arses and clutching breakfast tins of McEwan's Export. It's pretty safe to say the legendary climber John Norman Collie never had to endure any such sight in his latter years of life while staring out of these very same windows to reflect on his many accomplishments in this beloved mountain range. The hotel staff took a very dim view of the pair's actions as well and were fuming, but were pleasantly told where to go.

One group set off in the minibus for Glen Brittle on the south-western side of the range, but in doing so, disappeared with all the second group's boots, who, incredibly, set off for the climb wearing trainers! Sgùrr nan Gillean seemed to be the obvious choice for a starter as it was nearest, but no one had any real clue about where the most accessible route lay. The 'Tourist Path' is the accepted route, which most use to climb or descend, but it is certainly not for tourists with absolutely no sign of burger vans, ice cream parlours or Kiss-Me-Quick hats along the way. By some miracle, they managed to find themselves on it and, rather shakily and nervously, made their way to the very small and claustrophobic summit where vertiginous drops lay only a few feet away. This was a far cry from the usual hands-in-pockets, casual saunter of a hill walk and Johnny V Diff remembered thinking to himself, 'if it's like this ah day it's gonna be terrible.'

It was about to get a lot worse for the Cuillin rookies. Jake, who was a fellow worker in the factory, had only come along for a break from the house and some good old Scottish fresh air. He was no mountaineer and much more at home playing badminton in the local sports centre. The Bonnie Prince, JB and Mackie had a few hills under their belts, but nothing compared to these monstrous harbingers of rocky fear. Dougie Mac was the oldest in the group and took to the hands-on scrambling like a natural. He led them down the ultra-narrow and in places, fantastically exposed West Ridge, where any kind of a slip will most definitely end in death, a worrying thought that was never far from any man's mind.

At the time of writing, some 36 years had passed since this first Skye visit of the newer band and getting exact and accurate memories of routes taken proved sketchy and hazy. With no ropes, harnesses or slings and with a feeling they all may as well have done it blindfolded, such was the helpless feeling of the unknown. Dougie Mac's Tours had managed to lead them over Gillean, Am Bàisteir, Bruach na Frithe, the sensationally terrifying Bidein Druim nan Ramh and Sgùrr a' Mhadaidh before finally exiting via An Dorus. With certain sections graded Moderate to Difficult in climbing terms, it was a truly remarkable feat by the group for a first visit to Skye.

The day had not passed without incident, and on more than one occasion, at least one and sometimes all of them had experienced tidal waves of adrenaline and discomfort on the more exposed sections. Dougie Mac had a very lucky escape when he'd committed himself to a move and pulled on a rock, which in turn dislodged itself from the face. For a split second, he was overcome with fear and the dreaded thought that he was about to fall into mangled oblivion. Only some razor-sharp actions prevented this; he was able to stay in balance and calmly sidestep, letting the huge boulder crash down the mountain and shatter into smaller pieces as it went.

On another section, they were halted in their tracks by a gap in the ridge, which looked as if they might have to turn back, as the terrain all around was extremely precipitous with a massive drop into the abyss. Two seconds later, Dougie Mac went flying through the air and landed on a sloping rock at the other side. Cool as you like, he shouted to the rest who couldn't believe what they had just witnessed, 'mon ower lads, itz arite!'

The Bonnie Prince led the unanimous chorus back to Dougie with a forceful, 'Ya kin go an tak a flyin' fuck tae yirsel, wir no' jumpin' THAT ya maniac!'

'Well, if ya dinna, yir gonna hae tae back climb ah the difficulties wiv jist come ower,' he reasoned. This was true and planted some serious doubt into the others. After some nervous debate, one by one they all took the leap of faith, well nearly all. Badmington Jake had become cragfast and utterly frozen with fear and refused to make the jump. It was only after some time-consuming words of reassurance and psychological nurturing and telling him that he wouldn't die and would be laughing about it later in the pub that he finally donned the guise of Spiderman and jumped.

It was 8 o'clock in the evening by the time the weary and nerve-shredded group reached the Youth Hostel in Glen Brittle, and with no sign of their friends or the minibus, there was nothing else for it but to stick the thumbs out and start the huge walk back to Sligachan. A passing van very kindly agreed to take the hitchers to The Old Inn at Carbost, where they'd maybe be able to phone the Sligachan Hotel in the hope of getting someone to come and pick them up. It was near midnight before they eventually got back to the tents with bellies full of ale and tempers fraying – a full-scale punch-up was narrowly averted.

The following year saw most of the Skye debutants return with a hungry appetite for more Cuillin-ary mountain cuisine. One character was missing, however. Badmington Jake had had more than his fair share of jagged gabbro and hanging off sheer cliffs and had reverted to the much safer and horizontally level playing court in the gym, where the most danger on offer was from a possible shuttlecock to the face.

The club had found a new spot to rough camp at the side of the A863 road, a mile or so from the official Sligachan campsite. For those who remember, there used to be an old barn with a corrugated roof and a rusty old Lambretta scooter embedded into the earth. This would be the site of choice for many years to come and was well within staggering distance from the hotel bar.

The fabled In Pinn (Inaccessible Pinnacle), the notorious blade of basalt rock which rises above the summit of Sgùrr Dearg, is regarded by many hillwalkers as the hardest of all the Munros due to the unnerving exposure and sensational location where it is situated. The views of the Main Ridge from the summit on a clear day are truly awe-inspiring, if not a tad vertigo-inducing, as the feeling of being up in the gods is incredibly powerful. This was the target for the day, along with Sgùrr a' Mhadaidh and Sgùrr na Banachdich, and it was a full party who drove round in the minibus to begin the approach from An Dorus. Again, no climbing paraphernalia was anywhere to be seen. When they finally reached the top of Sgùrr Dearg, some of the group began to show signs of nervousness, with a little doubt starting to creep in.

Big Geordie (one half of the Dangerous Brothers) had a quick look, then set off up the short, near-vertical side, which is usually the recognised descent route via abseil. The rest watched with hearts in mouths as the big man carefully picked his way up before finally giving a fist pump at the top. As he went to descend down the long end, a party were coming up, tied onto a rope with jangly bits dangling from harnesses.

'Where the hell have you come from?' asked a rather bewildered climber.

'Ach eh jist climbed up the front an' ehm headin' doon here,' answered Geordie.

'You've no bloody rope or anything. You make us look like right muppets.' The guy was flabbergasted. Big Geordie gave a wee smile and a 'see ya' then skipped off down once they were all safely up. The waiting pals asked what it was like and was it ok to climb?

'Ach yull be fine, itz a wee bit narrow in places but nae baather,' and with that reassuring answer, they all successfully climbed up the east ridge then retraced their steps down. The mood in the Sliggy that night was one of untamed mayhem, as they had all completed something special and with that, the bevvy flowed harder, and the hilarity went a little too far. JB leapt up onto the pool table and was singing his heart out in harmony with the resident band while stomping his climbing boots in time on the green baize. This behaviour went down like a lead balloon with the bar staff, who duly ejected the stomper and banned the club from setting foot in there ever again.

'That's jist magic JB, ya complete erse. Wut we gonna dae next year?' complained Cliffy.

'Ach, wull git pished in Portree instead,' replied the guilty man. They did however return the following June and thankfully the bar staff had forgotten the incident, or the faces involved.

The Dangerous Brothers were no strangers to Skye and, during a couple of previous visits, had excelled on the testing terrain of the Main Ridge. On what was possibly their first visit, they had gone out to the southern end to start at Gars-bheinn and went all the way along to Sgùrr Alasdair. They had no ropes and just tackled whatever appeared before them, going up and over Caisteal a' Garbh-Choire (which is usually abseiled), then up and over the notorious Thearlaich Dubh Gap – or TD Gap as it is more widely known – all done in clumpy hillwalking boots. This deep cleft in the ridge is nearly always bypassed by standard hillwalkers and is left to those experienced in climbing and more often than not with the security of a rope. On questioning the pair later in the pub, Bruce, who'd done a fair bit of climbing and had a good knowledge of features on the ridge, asked them if they'd gone over the TD Gap, explaining it in detail.

'Well if thatz wut itz called then eh, we did it nae baather,' laughed Ronnie.

On another mad occasion (and rope-less once more), they'd gone up the 'Tourist Path' of Sgùrr nan Gillean and descended the exposed West Ridge, then up to the summit of Am Bàisteir. For most Munro baggers, the route would simply be reversed before carrying on round the path in Coire a' Bhasteir to Bruach na Frithe, but not the Dangerous Brothers. With a seemingly fearless attitude, they climbed into the unknown without really batting an eyelid or worrying about the imposing technicalities which the Basteir Tooth presented and down climbed very steep rock on the Lota Corrie side, which they had to climb 100 metres back up to regain the ridge. None of this was ever done out of bravado or having suicidal tendencies; they were just extremely comfortable on ground, which most hillwalkers would find incredibly mental.

A few of the newer members had their first taste of the Black Cuillin in the very early '90s and all week in the factory during the lead up to that meet, Wee Ecky, Big Betty and Tardy kept asking the now seasoned campaigners what it was really like and would they manage the challenges of exposed scrambling? Having completed only 20-odd 'standard' Munros of the round and rolling variety each and indulged in a wee practice scramble on Stùc a' Chròin in Perthshire two weeks previously, they were about to get the answer to all their questions in the form of a gabbro sledgehammer.

A full contingent of a dozen members were in attendance for the now popular annual meet and with the bus barely out of the car park in Dundee, the first few ring pulls could be heard bursting on the A90, bringing beer cans to life. Also travelling up in their car were the infamous Dangerous Brothers and Mackie, who were intent on tackling the whole ridge in one sustained effort. With a top-up of ale in the Kyle of Lochalsh, it was a jovial mob who boarded the ferry and began a cat's chorus of 'Speed Bonnie Boat' as they sailed over the sea to Skye. The occupants of the car would be leaving it with the main party and getting the bus driver to take them round to Glen Brittle. (We will follow this epic part of the story later.)

The hour was late, around 1.00am, when they staggered off the bus at the old barn and were greeted by a swarm of ferocious Hebridean midges. The air was peppered with expletives as men tried valiantly to erect tents in the unfair fight. Not to be put off, Big Betty (who had brought the pipes along to entertain the campers) appeared defiantly outside his tent and heaved and puffed to fire up the bag. The others stepped up to the mark with cans in hand, awaiting the melodic din to fill the air. Some other campers, who were stationed only 100 yards away, were not so keen to hear a 'cat being strangled' and complained that the hour was late and they were climbing mountains early tomorrow.

The end of their amplified sentences got drowned out and abandoned as the first notes of 'Bonnie Dundee' thundered out over the heathery landscape. Much whoopin' and hoochin' and choochin' belted out from the enthusiastic rabble, but the mood was in danger of turning rebellious as the tune petered out to a whine.

'Ho, wutz the crack? Wahrz the music?'

Big Betty, who was frantically wiping thousands of insects from his face and hands, fired back, 'Ehm gittin eaten alehv fae these ravenous wee bastirdz!'

'Never mind yir greetin', gaun rattle oot 'Heilan' Laddie' an' the 'Barren Rocks o' Aden' fir wih.'

And so, it went well until 3.00am and Big Betty could play no more due to his head inflating to the size of a large turnip from the multitude of bites. Sgùrr nan Gillean stood silently under the starry June twilight and wished them goodnight. She would be getting acquainted with some of them in a few hours time and ominously, showing her teeth to any who dared set foot on her rocky slopes.

Most of the early birds were up at 7.00am, slightly fuzzy-headed and reeking of alcohol, but keen to make the most of a beautiful sunny morning and by 8.00am, a group of six eager men were following Dougie Mac in the direction of Sgùrr nan Gillean while the rest headed round to Brittle. The excited chatter and banter soon fell silent as hands were employed to hold on to the ever-steepening rock. Stones and boulders began regularly raining down on the unfortunate stragglers at the back, dislodged by the clumsy boots of those who were further up. 'Crack o' Dawn' Colin shouted up to Dougie, 'are ya sure this is right, itz gittin affy steep?'

'Yep, eh mind o' this fae last year. Jist keep headin' up an' wull be on the summit in nae time,' replied Dougie calmly.

They were, in fact, unknowingly climbing straight up the technically demanding 'Pinnacle Ridge' and the sound of bottles crashing from the Skye virgins within the party was becoming deafening. The phrase 'ehm shitin' meh breeks' was almost becoming a mantra as fear began to dominate all but the mind of Dougie, who seemed to be breezing over any difficulties and was totally oblivious to any huge drops. By the time they reached the summit of the notorious third pinnacle of 'Knight's Peak', Dougie's apprentices were consumed by sheer terror and a feeling of impending death, made all the more sinister as the lovely, clear skies had given way to a thick and swirling mist with sheets of fine drizzle.

A climbing party were already on the now overcrowded summit and were setting up an abseil. One of them shouted over, 'Where's your ropes and gear lads?'

Dougie fired back, 'Ach we dinna hae any o' that shite, wull find a weh doon.'

The reply from the climber was chilling in its delivery. 'Well good luck lads, we'll see you in hospital or maybe the morgue.'

The mood in the group was becoming ever more desperate, and the prospect of retreat brought even more waves of fear. Dougie, however, was having none of it and off he went like a crab shimmying along a sharp ridge into the Coire a' Bhàsteir side. The drop here is horrendous but was thankfully hidden by the thick swirling mist. One by one, each man followed Dougie's lead and leapt into a small gully before clambering over to where the main man was perched, howling with laughter. Shortly afterwards, they finally reached the small summit of Gillean. Very little words were spoken as nerves were shot to pieces. 'Crack o' Dawn' Colin was literally shittin' his breeks and had to relieve himself just below where the group were gathered to have a piecey break. The silence was broken when someone shouted, 'Aw Jesus Christ, kin ya no' go an' dae that sumwahr else, itz fuckin' reekin!'

'Eh good ane, ehm hingin' on here fir grim death an' strugglin' tih wipe ma erse! Ehl tell yiz wut, ehv parachuted oot o' planes an' been in helicopters wi' the army but eh huv NEVER been on anything as insane as this fuckin' hill!'

Visibility was very poor when the Pied Piper called on his Cuillin Rats to follow in the direction of the West Ridge. Dark pointed rocks reared menacingly ahead in the mist and, at one point, Dougie jumped over a gap on the ridge, encouraging the others to follow. The men went into mutiny and refused as they stared down into the abyss. Dougie jumped back over, and they retraced their steps to the summit, not having a clue on which way lay the safest descent. Somewhere, possibly on the Coire a' Bhàsteir side, the Pied Piper shouted back to the men, 'Wiv cracked it lads, ehv found a scree shoot, wull be doon in nae time.'

The scree shoot petered out very quickly and they ended up on a slanting ledge, having to duck down below a huge overhang, with the way ahead getting narrower and narrower. Loose stones went over the edge and were not heard landing for what seemed like a very long time, which meant they were on some cliff face. Once more, they returned to the summit and, by sheer luck, they found the 'Tourist Path' or did they? Wherever it was, they made it down and that night in the Sliggy, the bevvy tasted all the more sweeter as they raised a toast to 'still being alive'.

The other groups shared similar stories of crazy route-finding from round on the Glen Brittle side, but nothing compared to the epic, which involved the Dangerous Brothers and Mackie, who were making an attempt on the whole ridge. On the Friday night from the Brittle car park, they had kept walking into the wee small hours and bivvyed at the foot of Gars-bheinn. Sleep, however, was virtually non-existent as their sweating bodies soon cooled in the bivvy bags and they were left shivering with teeth chattering like machine guns. After a while, the discomfort proved too much, and the decision was made to crack on. Their efforts, however, were rewarded with a beautiful sunrise once they gained the Main Ridge. This time, there would be no gung-ho risk-taking and they had brought climbing gear and an ancient hemp rope that had belonged to Ronnie's dad. The first hold-up happened on 'The Castle' when the rope got stuck after abseiling and Big Geordie had to climb back up to free it.

At Sgùrr Dubh an Da Bheinn, they dropped their packs at a col before scrambling up to Sgùrr Dubh Mòr. On the return, however, they couldn't find the packs and spent an age looking for them before finally stumbling on them. The view to the west was giving cause for concern as a huge band of cloud and sea mist was rolling in at an alarming rate and would soon envelope them. (This same weather front, which caused the problems for the others).

The next major obstacle came at TD Gap, which by now was soaking wet and would be a huge challenge to surmount. Repeated attempts proved fruitless on the dangerously slippy, polished surface and the decision was taken to traverse over to Bealach Sgumain, then gain the summit of Sgùrr Alasdair. In the thick rolling mist and drizzle, they had somehow overshot the intended route and ended up on some extremely exposed terrain on the Coire Lagan side. To make matters worse, the trio got split up and each man would later retell his own battle for survival on the face. Desperate shouts to locate each other were swallowed up and drowned out in the howling wind. They were also acutely aware that any mistake would cost them their lives. Big Geordie remembered crawling along a ledge, his hands and knees shredded and bleeding as he faked anxiously in the mist for some escape out of the hell he'd found himself in.

It was a greatly relieved group of friends who, one by one, eventually found each other on the tiny summit of Sgùrr Alasdair, where each man told of their nerve-shattering personal battles for self-preservation. Right there and then would be the perfect moment where the majority of 'normal' walkers would be calling it quits and making the sharp exit down the Great Stone Shoot, especially after the epic which these three had just endured. But this was the Dangerous Brothers and Mackie (who was no stranger to danger himself and would, in fact, become a fully-fledged member of the Dangerous Brothers in the following years) and, without a second thought for the enormity of the task in front of them or the worsening weather, they carried on up Sgùrr Thearlaich and back onto the Main Ridge.

Route-finding had become nigh on impossible as they tried to get down to the Bealach Mhic Choinnich (which is difficult even in clear weather), and the decision was sensibly made to abort the attempt on the whole ridge. Much time had already been lost and it was now mid-afternoon. They had one very obvious and serious problem; there was no safe escape route unless they went all the way back to Sgùrr Thearlaich and abseiled down to the Great Stone Shoot. Ronnie Mac took the bull by the horns and, in keeping with Dangerous Brothers' traditions, simply said, 'Ach wull jist head doon here.' The 'here' he was referring to was another huge face down the Coire Lagan side, and off they went on what was another complete nightmare descent.

By the time they reached the Glen Brittle car park Big Geordie and Mackie were knackered and the prospect of having to walk back to Sligachan, some nine miles, filled them with utter dread. Ronnie Mac, who was fit as a fiddle at the time, told his pals to rest up while he ran all the way back to get the car and in no time at all, he was back to get them, where they soon joined the others in the bar for a night of shared stories and drunken shenanigans.

On 16 October 1995, the final ferry sailed between the Kyle of Lochalsh on the mainland and Kyleakin on the Isle of Skye, and in doing so marked the end of an era, which stretched back hundreds of years. It was a sad day for locals and tourists alike as it coincided with the opening of the brand new Skye Bridge, which was to become a fiery and contentious issue for the next nine years or so due to the toll charges. It did, of course, mean a quicker journey over to the island, but the romanticism of the ferry trip was lost forever. When departing the island, the Club did (and still does) try to use and support the other ferry at Kylerhea, which crosses to the lovely village of Glenelg and has been operating for 100s of years. It does, of course, boast the MV Glenachulish, the last manually operated turntable ferry in the world and a forward journey which takes the traveller over the stunning Mam Ratagan Pass.

In the summer of 1999, the club was actually grateful for the Skye Bridge as the minibus was on a mission to get to Sligachan pronto and get the tents up in readiness for a trip up to Portree and the Gathering Hall. The reason was a highly anticipated gig by the late and legendary dreadlocked piper and musical genius, Martyn Bennett. The club had become good friends with Martyn, and as the self-titled 'Dundee Bennetteers', they had sought to follow him where and when they could across Scotland to immerse themselves in his unique brand of hypnotic and chaotic Folk/Techno/Scottish/Dance anthems. These events were always a sweaty explosion of uncontrolled jigging carnage where the drink flowed as swiftly as the notes flying out of the chanter.

And so, when Martyn alerted the gang to the forthcoming event, the timing could not have been any better as it was the annual Skye weekender. The forecast was atrocious with the threat of torrential rain, but all was dry and well (and miraculously stayed that way for the whole weekend!) as the tents were erected in double quick time before the small fleet of taxis sped up to Portree. Martyn was there to greet the lads with beer in hand and was equally excited to get the thoughts and feedback from the new sound he was about to unleash. His smiling face on stage was a sure sign that things were going just great as the audience stomped, birled, reeled and bounced while oiling their throats. At the end of the show, the NCR boys were slaughtered. Bodies were scattered everywhere as some found their way to the burger van while others swallow-dived into taxis. Big Betty's old man had been in a taxi then pressed the ejector seat and got out to look for his son, who was by now passing and had seen his dad now crawling out of a phone box. He would make it back to camp... eventually.

The fact that any of them made it out of their sleeping bags in the morning was a true miracle to behold. Nine men stood on parade, still staggering and stuttering while contemplating the serious challenge of climbing Sgùrr Mhic Chòinnich. The stiff scrambling up to the airy summit had the adrenaline levels fired to the max and proved the perfect tonic for a detox. One man, however, was quietly sitting there, not daring to look down at the huge drops surrounding them and, if truth be told, he was absolutely shitting his breeks. The bold Sir Lancelot (so named because of his uncanny resemblance to a famous medieval knight) would be the first to admit he had never been comfortable with exposure and the thought of returning down the narrow ridge filled him with sheer terror. He was near the front of the group descending when he came to an abrupt halt and began dry humping a large rock, refusing to go any further. He had become cragfast and point-blank refused to move.

Pity was never high on the agenda within the club when any climber's bottle began to crash and sympathy was even lower down the pecking order. With black humour in abundance, each man who had to squeeze past Lancelot turned the dry humper into the dry humpee as they simulated 'rogering' him from behind. The gallant knight became a quivering wreck as the party mocked and ridiculed their poor brother, who only decided to shakily continue after they threatened to leave him up there for the night.

On arrival back at camp, they were met with the unzipping of a tent flap and a familiar face peeking his head out.

'Arite lads,' said Fred. 'Wut are we goin' fir the day?' Keen as ever to get a hill done.

'Awa ya daft erse,' replied Joe. 'It's FOUR IN THE EFTERNANE an' yiv missed the boat!'

Everyone fell around laughing as Fred realised he had slept all night and most of the day. That's what a Bennett gig could do to some.

There was a celebratory party in the Sligachan Hotel that night as the big man mountain (who used to do the door), had recently completed the herculean effort of rowing a large boat over The Minch for a local charity. The NCR boys didn't need any encouragement for a second night of mayhem and went full throttle once more. Big Betty's dad was still suffering from the Friday night and had taken his leave earlier, but not before buying some raffle tickets. He was sound asleep in his tent when his number was called, and he was now the proud owner of a bottle of whisky – a bottle which he would never see. The guardians of the said bottle were last spotted at 3.00am passing it around themselves till there wasn't a drop left. Those same guardians were then chauffeured down to Loch Slapin only a few hours later, where the 'Water o' Life' allegedly helped propel them up Bla Bheinn. Other reports more accurately cited that they were all still steaming and were crawling up it.

Like many others before him in the club, Joe was now about to become a Munro Compleatist and had chosen the shapely peak of Sgùrr Dubh Mòr as his last. Any final summit party was always highly anticipated and as this was Skye, the minibus was packed to capacity and the members were in higher spirits than usual, if that was at all possible.

The weather gods had been kind and had delivered a dry and warm day for the party as they snaked their way up Coire a' Ghrunnda and onto the Main Ridge. In the past, it was traditional to crack open the champagne and whisky for any final summit soiree, but as this peak required a fair degree of exposed scrambling and concentration, it was decided to save the drinking until after the job was done and they returned to some safer ground. One by one, the large group assembled on the narrow summit to salute Joe's magnificent achievement and congratulate the man of the moment. Big Betty took the pipes from his rucksack and fired into a celebratory rendition of 'Cock o' the North' but soon had to sit down to play them after complaining of dizziness and vertigo. The puffing and blowing had caused some lightheadedness and he said that he felt as if he was going to fall to his death. The ongoing hangover may have had a small part to play in these morbid feelings of doom during such a joyous occasion.

When they returned safely to Sgùrr Dubh an Da Bheinn they wasted no time in setting about the carry-outs where drams were raised, champagne was popped and then hastily downed to be quickly refilled. The effects from their earlier exertions mixed with bubbles and malt produced a rapid tipsy feeling, but this was of no concern as the plan was to descend the fairly easy route, which they had come up. Following a few more drams, someone suggested a 'much quicker route' over the ridge of Sgùrr Sgumain and down the Sgumain Stone Shoot. And with that statement, any clear thinking and sensible decision-making got booted right into touch as the giggling band donned their rucksacks and staggered off below the towering bulk of Sgùrr Alasdair in search of this 'quick descent'.

On gaining the Sgumain Ridge, they surveyed the view down into Coire Lagan, which looked dangerously steep and wholly uninviting. Three men departed up Alasdair while the rest followed a trickle of small stones, which must indeed be the Stone Shoot. They were, in fact, nowhere near it and about to head down the same huge face that the Dangerous Brothers had clung onto for dear life previously. The giggling and banter soon gave way to frantic grunting and cursing as each man fought desperately to stay attached to the rock. At the water's edge of the idyllic Lochan Coire Lagan, all eyes gazed back in horror at what they had just descended, then a kangaroo court was hastily set up to try the guilty man who had made the outrageous route suggestion in the first place.

It was Joe who settled the nerves and produced a bottle of finest Scottish malt whisky from his rucksack and offered it up to the gods for sparing their lives. With no gods taking up Joe's generous offer, it was left to the men to pass around continuously until the bottle was well and truly wrung out. With a glow back on each climber's face, it was a jovial and very grateful bunch who descended the track to Brittle and were soon completely focused on the forthcoming Saturday night festivities and a proper shindig.

For some reason, the annual pilgrimage to Skye seemed to produce hard and epic battles on the mountains and equally hard and epic sessions on the drink. It must surely have been the overwhelming excitement of travelling to an island where life is a whole lot different to that of the city. It also had the added bonus of the best and most challenging mountains in the entire British Isles. Early climbing pioneers had become famous, some having mountains named after them, while others left their mark on some of the classic and most recognised routes in the Black Cuillin. One man even had a bench named in his honour, which we will get to shortly.

The group who had gone on this particular meet was a real mixture of experience and those who were raw and keen but hungry to get the necessary ticks to enhance their Munro tally. The jewel in the crown for most of the rookie party was to summit the Inaccessible Pinnacle, arguably the most sought after and nerve-jangling of all the peaks on the Baggers' list. A crash-course on abseiling was carried out prior to the trip on the Lundie Crags, situated just to the west of Dundee. This was conducted by one of the members who had some ropework and climbing experience and was simply passing on his knowledge. Memorising all that was being said and the various techniques to tie onto a harness and descend safely was of paramount importance. Get it wrong when you are on your own on the In Pinn and you are most likely very dead.

That's really how it was in the club, learning on the feet and go for it, with a bit of nerves and a lot of bottle. Nobody had hundreds of pounds to employ a guide to pull them over the various objectives and to be fair, no one even contemplated the thought.

The weather was fair but held a blustery wind as the large group scrambled up and onto the summit of Sgùrr Dearg from the west to assemble below the In Pinn. A party consisting of a guide with clients was already preparing their gear and roping up in readiness for the climb. For one of the NCR boys, it was now or never as he had shat himself in the very same spot the year before and bottled it. Big Betty took a deep breath, composed himself then began the assault on the Pinn along with the others, scrambling freely up the narrow arete of the long end until they reached the top. The midweek training paid off as each man successfully negotiated the descent, then continued on to Banachdich, Ghreadaidh and Mhadaidh before exiting via An Dorus. Johnny V Diff had struck up a conversation on the Ridge with a party of English climbers, who were attempting the whole traverse, so he decided he'd like to continue with them, thus cheerio's were said and off he went.

That night in the Sligachan Hotel can only be described as complete carnage as the chimp's tea party went into celebration mode following a very successful day. The NCR held court at the large table in the centre of the packed bar, like a wild Viking mob returning from a raiding party. Cammy (who was the club's 'Weekend Meet Secretary' at the time and held in very high esteem) had turned up wearing an outfit which some remarked as 'looking like German lederhosen attire'. This prompted him to go goose-stepping up and down the length of the bar in the style of Basil Fawlty from the 1970s comedy series *Fawlty Towers*. By the time V Diff arrived with his newfound English companions (all still in climbing gear and had to abort at Am Bàisteir due to extreme fatigue) at 10.30pm, he was greeted with a boisterous but friendly riot while having to dodge flying ice-cubes. He couldn't believe these were the same people he had been conversing sanely with only a few hours earlier.

At closing time, they poured out into the darkened car park and with the bite of the fresh midnight air came a sure reminder of how much alcohol had been sunk. Speech turned to slur and walk turned to stagger as men fumbled desperately for a sense of direction towards the tents pitched up at the old barn. Big Betty spotted a bench and decided he was going to lift it, so he did. The solid frame weighed a ton on his head as he valiantly fought to steady himself.

'Dinna worry lads,' he bawled to no one, 'ehv got us a bench tae sit on at the campsite.'

The campsite was a mile up the road, but waver, stumble and stagger as he did, he accepted no offers of help. This was man against bench and there was no way on this earth he was going to be beaten. Slowly but not-so-surely, each man fell into camp one by one. Big Betty was fairly chuffed with his night's work but did complain to anyone who would listen that his scalp was now throbbing with deep indentations from bench spars. He got no sympathy. Someone shone a head torch onto the bench to read the small plaque, which went something like 'In memory of renowned British mountain photographer and guidebook writer William Arthur Poucher (1891–1988)'.

'Hey, ehv heard o' that boy, he's pretty famous.'

'Nah, never heard o' uhm. Eez bench is comfy though.'

As men agreed and disagreed how famous the old boy was, Farfar returned from his tent with a bottle of red wine and all hell let loose.

'Aw ya dancer! Mair swally. Hurry up an' git it open.'

A corkscrew was found and passed to the man from Forfar, who proceeded to miss the cork and put it straight through his hand. While he screamed in agony and winced at the blood pouring out, Cammy took on the job and got the plonk open to loud cheers. Any good wine connoisseur will tell you that a nice bottle of red should be left to breathe at room temperature before consuming, but this poor thing was decimated in a matter of minutes. It went back to Cammy, who swigged the last mouthful then tossed it recklessly into the night. This would be the most expensive wine he ever tasted in his life.

In the morning, the campsite was a hive of activity as voices were raised amid a huge inquest into the previous night's antics. Big Betty awoke just in time to hear his name being mentioned in Judge Johnny V Diff's kangaroo court.

'Eh that drunken bastird's panned (smashed) the bus windee in!'

Big Betty had to wrestle through a pile of rocks and crawl under Mr Poucher's bench, which had been rammed up against his tent door by some comedian, just to protest his innocence. Following some extensive detective work, an empty wine bottle was found at the front of the minibus, which had been lobbed over the old barn and the last hands on it were those of the Weekend Meet Secretary. With full excess to pay, Cammy's wallet was £180 lighter, which was a huge amount to a common factory worker in 1996. How the driver was able to steer the bus all the way back to Dundee through the shattered spider's web of glass was anybody's guess, but he did.

(Homage was paid to Wullie Poucher's bench with a full ceremonial service before being returned completely unharmed to its rightful location in the Sligachan car park.)

Our final small tale from the Misty Isle involved an epic error of judgment from one member who really should have known better but whose straight thinking was lost in the haze of many malts a few hours earlier as the group celebrated a great day on the Main Ridge then watched on as Ray Houghton secured a win for Ireland versus Italy at the 1994 Football World Cup finals. This trip was different to all the previous ones as some brave Day Meet walkers had attended in the hope of being led over some of the Cuillin giants, and they weren't disappointed as they held on for dear life while scaling the exposed bulk of Clach Glas on route to the summit of Bla Bheinn. A few of the newbies were in danger of freaking out completely and losing their nerve altogether during the various technical scrambling sections. In fairness, these fellow club members were much more at home strolling over some of the more rounded and grassy hills in Scotland and it took Cammy to show some excellent leadership skills and inspire them to overcome their fears when it mattered most.

Give them their due, they were up sharp on the Sunday morning and keenly heading with many of the seasoned campaigners for another challenging and scary day on the West Ridge of Sgùrr nan Gillean. One man, however, was not up sharp and awoke mid-morning, still half-canned, to find the tents deserted. Although rough as a rhino's arse, Big Betty was not one for wasting a hill day on Skye, especially as the June sunshine was already radiating warm rays, so he hastily and rather unsteadily readied himself and headed in the direction of the mass of Glamaig over on the Red Cuillin to stretch the legs. With a mouth as dry as the bottom of a budgie's cage, he had only made it as far as the River Sligachan and a spot just down from the hotel. He filled his bottle and greedily gulped down the cool, crystal clear (or so he thought) water before refilling and setting off to bag the summit.

If he could have had a crystal ball, a large helping of hindsight, a functioning brain and a microscope, he may well have seen that the 'crystal clear water' was, in fact, crawling with a million gruesome bacteria, who had left a multitude of arses from the hotel toilets, had swam down the shitey pipe to deposit into the river and a cruise on Loch Sligachan. The steep bouldery ascent in the blazing hot sun had Big Betty sweating buckets of last night's poison and stopping on numerous occasions to praise one of life's precious free gifts in outdoor Scotland – cool, fresh water.

'This is absolute nectar,' he thought, as the excrement blend slid down his throat while he gorged on the magnificent Inner Hebridean vista. Some 8 hours later, there was what can only be described as a volcanic eruption in a tenement in Dundee as Big Betty endured the full brunt of severe gastroenteritis, which culminated in a visit to nearby Ninewells Hospital and being wired up to various heart monitors. The more detailed events of what followed have thankfully been censored.

The Skye epics on and off the mountain were plentiful and in all honesty continue to this day, but for now, we shall leave the island in some kind of peace.

Hale Bop an' a Fosbury Flop

A bus bound fir Charlie country, the 'Bonnie Prince' that is
Visions o' romantic wanderin's, wahr once the Young Pretender wiz
Although 'he' wiz chasin' a Crown, an' 'they' wir daein it fir leisure
An' he had grim reaper Cumberland, pursuin' a 30-grand treasure
They wir pursuin' a ragin' thirst, an' damned if that thirst wid wait
The driver wiz threatened wi' GBH, 'Spean Bridge, Commando Bar mate!'
The bothy conquistadors swalleyed gung-ho, alang wi' some foamin' ale
Then a hard joab jemmyin' them fae the bar, tae kerry on the trail

'Ehv been tae Essan afore, itz straight alang the railway'
But that ramshackle human freight train, had spent too lang at the ceilidh
The rucksack carriages rocked an' rolled, an' teetered on the brink
An' Flyin' Scotsmen flew arite! Caused beh the bliddee drink
'Mind wir on Mallaig Main Drag, fir Christ sake, waatch fir trains!'
But danger wuzna bein' absorbed, into the pickled brains
'Wahr the hell's this bothy?' Came the mantra fae impatience
The lads derailed at Checkpoint Charlie, tae enter Essan Station

April showers wir aff on holiday, an' deep blue sky wore a sun
An' mountain men paid a penalty high, fir water o' which there wiz none
Amoeba-filled stagnant pools, wir ah the hills could submit
The taste bore sweet resemblance, tae the syllables 'sh' and 'it'
Still, three Corbetts wuzna bad, an' nane o' them ca'd Ronnie
Fae Rois-Bheinn's eyes oot tae the west – a panorama sae bonnie
An' Jacobite folklore ah aroond, fae Loch nan Uamh tae Moidart
Wi' strains o' 'Will Ye No' Come Back Again', pullin' on the heart

The day had been a belter, even wi' the septic water
An' springtime in the Western Highlands, couldna get much hotter
But backs wir patted premature, on the final homeward descent
A barbed sting fae a serpent's tail, led confidence tae dent
The bothy sat there laughin' smug, while they played gemmes wi' fear
Danglin' scared fae Heather's roots, on crags that ended sheer
Nervous laughter biled ower, fae a pot o' adrenaline soup
As Terry Firma finally comforted, in the Essan chicken coop

Tea never touched the sides, as the bar came under threat
An' part-time lunatics dressed in glad rags, fir a gemme o' Essan roulette
Arcadia wiz soon obliterated, as mayhem took a grip
Soon men wir talkin' total bumf, as the fire cracked her whip
The congregation sang 'Hosanna', tae a Highland malt piss-alm
An' gibbered pigeon-Hungarian, while parleyin' wi' a dram
An orgy o' drunken merriment, but no' the Roman type
Nah, this wiz jungle bothy law, wi' apocalyptic hype

Night danced a moonie ootside, wi' a dame ca'd Crystal Clear
When sumdee oot there takkin a leak, urged them tae 'Come here'
The perty staggered on the lawn, wi' glazed eyes starin' high
An' witnessed comet Hale Bop, blazin' through the sky
Some men stood in wonderment, while ithers stood in shite
A stray foot in a deer's latrine, nearly spoilt the historical sight
'Meh hade feels like that comet, tearin' aroond in space!'
A sentiment echoed by the mannequin platoon, ah wearin' a dummy's face

Back inside the Hydra's nest, wi' many mooths tae feed
The bottles did the roonds again, fir them that wir in need
Beh now, Big Fred wiz strugglin', an' sportin' a thousand yard stare
One flew ower the cuckoo's nest, as he sat there waashin eez hair
An ancient pagan ritual? Well it certainly hud men stumped
He rubbed eez hade like a crystal ball, nursin' it as it thumped
Then vertigo on a chair set in, a feelin' he couldna stop
The judges handed oot 'straight 10's, fir a fireside Fosbury Flop

Luckily, the stane hearth broke eez fall, an' eez bones remained intact
Stretchered straight tae eez sleepin' bag, fir a blind drunk pillow pact
Disordered chaos wiz restored, wi' a crash behind thir backs
Arkan scattered a table o' stoves, in an 'under-the-influence' collapse
Bothy orderlies wir workin' flat oot, tae tend the maimed an' needy
Jist casualties o' alcohol Armageddon, the price o' bein too greedy
Tough mountain men bowled ower, like skittles o' cotton wool
Ejected pronto fae the hootenanny, twa losers in a moonshine duel

Sunday, back on Mallaig Main Drag, but this train wiz nae express
The lads snaked oot o' Essan bothy, a broken human mess
Fred an' Arkan jist couldna recall, how last night's lights went oot
'Stop bungee-jumpin' aff tables an' chairs, thatz yir problem's root!'
Any sufferin' though wiz soon forgot, in a hostelry in Mallaig
Wahr 'hair o' the doag' wiz ordered up, which left the barmaid vague
An' up in space flew Hale Bop, lookin' doon on the crew
She whispered tae them, 'I'll be back,' an' then a kiss she blew.

This was a first visit to Essan bothy for many of the club members involved and proved unforgettable in so many ways. Situated on the south side of Loch Eilt, it lies in a stunning location below a backdrop of wonderfully rugged Corbetts to the west of Glenfinnan, with the towns of Arisaig and Mallaig continuing further on via the A830 road and the famous West Highland railway line. The main problem is getting there, as the loch, river and horrendous terrain stands in the way of any short, direct approach. Back then, (and the few occasions since) the decision was made without any doubt or worry, to walk the 3 miles or so from the west end of the loch along the railway, not legal and certainly not recommended in the black of night with full weekend packs and a wild session in the boozer beforehand but hey ho, that's the way it went.

The three Corbetts of Sgùrr na Ba Glaise, An Stac and Rois-Bheinn gave the party a strenuous challenge and, indeed, a dehydrating one as the only water to be had was from a stagnant and manky pool on the ridge which Big Flatters keenly drank from while the rest spectated, politely declined and duly boked at the thought, mindful of lingering hangovers. Deep blue and clear April skies rewarded them with some of the most breathtaking views anywhere in Scotland, but the return rollercoaster journey and subsequent crazy steep descent to the bothy soon had the group holding on for dear life.

Not all attendees on that particular meet had chosen to climb the mountains (even with a spectacular forecast) and a small breakaway band of rebels opted for a walk back out to the road and an all-dayer in the hostelries of Mallaig. The fireside soiree was in full swing and Hale Bop comet was bopping through a billion stars when a train pulled up outside the bothy to deposit a human cargo of drunken delinquents who tripped, staggered and cursed the few hundred yards back to the sanctuary of Essan before joining the raging party. These, of course, were the carefree days before health and safety went into namby-pamby overdrive and a five pound note or a half bottle of whisky placed in the right hand could get you dropped off at a desired location by a kind train driver. Highland hospitality at its absolute finest.

For those who witnessed Fred's sickening face plant into the hearth of the fire, the main worry was thinking he must be dead, while the next worry was how to stretcher his large carcass all the way back to the car park. Miraculously, he escaped without so much as a scratch on his body and only a walloping hangover the next morning.

During a festive excursion to the bothy, the NCR boys were enjoying some craic around the fire when three older guys from Glasgow entered, one of them looking positively knackered after lugging in an accordion. (Echoes of the late and legendary Tom Patey, who was known to lug his squeeze box on some marathon jaunts.) Following a couple of first-class mountain days and bothy nights, both parties left together for the slog back out along the railway. The pace varied considerably according to the 'hangover-ometer' and there, pulling up the rear, was the poor old guy lugging his faithful accordion.

He stopped and sat down for a breather saying, 'That's it, ah'm knackered,' then a few moments later added, 'Ach, ah'll tell yiz wut, ah'll gie yiz a wee tune.' And there he sat, trackside in the middle of nowhere, fingers firing into a frenzy as he gave a unique and impromptu, mini-ceilidh performance. As if on cue, two minutes later, the Mallaig to Fort William train could be heard rattling along the track, getting ever closer while the old guy kept squeezing for all he was worth. Joe did, in fact, witness the whole scene playing out and howled with laughter as he watched the faces in the carriages stare in disbelief at some lunatic perform a virtuoso gig. They must have thought they were in Brigadoon. Imaginations run riot to think what some of these tourists must have relayed back to family and friends when they got home.

CHAPTER 11

Is There Anybody There?

'The bothy's miles awa!'

SCOTTISH FOLKLORE HAS always been richly entwined with mythical figures, ghostly sightings and tales from the dark side weaving haunting and supernatural images that plant fear in our minds. But then, they are just made-up stories which have grown arms and legs over the years creating spooky visions which may send shivers down the spine when told in the shadowy and atmospheric setting round a fire in a candle lit bothy. Of course, they are not real. Or are they?

The human brain is a very powerful organ which, in certain circumstances can distort and encourage overwhelming feelings of terror due to possibly hearing something or seeing something. The logical and the sceptical among us will always argue there is an answer and reason for things which happen. But then there were hardened sceptics within the characters of which you are about to read, tough, no-nonsense working-class mountain men who didn't get spooked easily but would later admit to quivering under the protection of a flimsy sleeping bag and wishing it was morning.

Joe was a fully paid up member of the above gang, a man who

had been to countless bothies on his own, in the dark, in winter, in howling storms and would always ask the rest, 'If ya do see a ghost, wut the hell is it gonna dae tae ya? Scare ya tae death sayin' Woooooooh? A load o' aald shite if ya waant meh opinion.' And that's how he perceived any talk of supernatural drivel. That is until one visit to Coire Fionnaraich bothy way over in the north-west.

It was a full platoon, which left Coulags late one Friday night for the short march up to the bothy with one or two in the party a little worse for wear, having over-indulged on the long journey north. The bold Sir Lancelot was one of the guilty drunks and duly arrived at the abode minus his bag of coal. A kangaroo court was quickly assembled, and an intense round of interrogation began. The slavering medieval man strongly protested his innocence, giving the feeble excuse that he had fallen off the track and lost his supply in the dark. The judge let him off with a stern warning and the threat of a sound kicking and a wedgie if it happened again.

The fire in the main room was sparked into life and quickly brought some warmth to the chilly but well insulated place while most of the group set their sleeping bags out upstairs. Joe and Scottie opted for the adjacent downstairs room in the hope of avoiding the snoring chorus and the inevitable volleys of indiscriminate farting. Eventually, the fireside gathering got into the swing of things and the usual banter and micky-taking kicked off, interrupted by the odd folk song and refilling of drams. Outside, the old rowan tree danced and creaked in the stiff breeze. Sadly, this tree no longer stands on the front lawn, no doubt callously cut down by some lunatic and fed into the fire. It is said that the rowans were the chosen species of tree, specifically planted by their original tenants outside these isolated cottages to ward off any evil spirits.

During the proceedings, Johnny V Diff decided to have a spring clean of the bothy and any burnable rubbish was thrown onto the fire. Some ancient, tattered and manky thermal jacket hung on a peg by the door and duly fell into the 'rubbish' category, so it too joined the flame. Whatever the garment was made of was highly flammable and soon had the lum roaring like a runaway express train, but thankfully, it burnt itself out and normal service was resumed with no need for any man to become an amateur firefighter. Final drams were sunk as the embers died in the fire and the last of the revellers retired to their cosy sleeping bags.

At some point in the wee small hours, Joe was woken by the sound of pots clanking over in the far corner of the room and he sheepishly rubbed his eyes to try to see who it was in the semi-gloom. A shiver ran the length of his body and he froze as he saw the outline of an 'old lady' moving around erratically. This went on for what seemed like an age, but in reality it was maybe around five to ten seconds before she vanished and an orb began to glow and fly about the room. His mate Scottie slept soundly by his side, but by now, Joe was gripped with fear and withdrew his head tightly under the safety of his sleeping bag. The rest of his night was highly restless and he fell in and out of sleep. He remembers hearing knocking noises and the distinct sound of someone clumping down the wooden staircase, unhooking the door latch and going outside, but they never returned. (No one had, in fact, gone out that night.)

In the morning, he said not a word to anyone, gathered all his gear and relocated to a room upstairs. Unaware of any goings-on but certainly not wanting to sleep in the cold, grey room on his own, Scottie followed his friend.

That day, the men split into small groups and went their own ways, passing the nearby Clach nan Con-fionn (the stone of Fingal's dogs, where the legendary giant is reputed to have tethered his dogs) before tackling the Munro circuit of Maol Chean-dearg, Beinn Liath Mhòr and An Sgùrr Ruadh, while others went to the impressive Corbetts of Fuar Tholl and An Ruadh-stac. Still, Joe held his silence and never muttered a word about what he had encountered the previous night.

Back at the bothy, the main room was filled with excited chat as men discussed their day's adventures while cooking up some curried cuisine, when Big Betty suddenly shouted to the others, 'GIT OOT THE WEH! MA COOKER'S GONNA EXPLODE!' He hadn't screwed the gas cannister on properly and flames were now escaping out of the fitting. He picked it up and flew out the door like a madman before tossing it into the night. It didn't explode, but the possibility of it going off in a packed room didn't bear thinking about.

Following the earlier drama, the night was going like a fair round the roaring fire when something very odd happened. Four of the men who had their backs to the wall where the staircase climbed behind, stopped what they were doing for a second, then turned to look at each other. Big Geordie broke the silence first and quietly asked Wee Ecky, 'Did you hear that?'

'Yeah, eh heard a wummin screamin' fae behind us,' he answered. The other two said exactly the same thing as a cold shiver ran straight down their spines. For those who didn't hear it, it was scoffed at and generally shot down in a round of piss-taking. Joe sat rather agitated, listening to the others, but made no comment. The night carried on as any other Saturday bothy night did and no more sounds or happenings were reported. It wasn't until Sunday morning when they were walking back out to Coulags and Coire Fionnaraich was well behind them, when Joe finally shared his experience of Friday night in the other room and the terror he had felt. 'Sumhin definitely wuzna right in there, an' that wiz WITH the rowan tree lookin' efter us,' he said, and with that statement, his days of scepticism were well and truly over.

The snow was falling heavier and thicker by the minute and the large flakes were becoming mesmerising in the minibus headlights as a party of eight passed through Crianlarich heading west for a weekend's rough camping in Glen Etive. Conditions quickly turned into a full-blown blizzard and the driver complained of struggling to make out anything which remotely resembled a road in the total whiteness. There was a real fear among the men that the meet would have to be aborted, but they slowly crawled on till they reached the sanctuary of the Bridge Of Orchy Hotel, where a meeting was hastily called. This, of course, led to a few pints and drams, which in turn led to a great many more and a rowdy sing-song to boot. There was no let-up with the wild weather and Glen Etive was now well and truly off the menu. Driving the 14 miles or so down the winding single-track road would have been suicidal, so the bunkhouse was booked and more lashings of ale and malt followed.

The morning couldn't have dawned any more differently as the snow had given way to heavy rain and incredibly, the road was now clear. After a hearty round of full Scottish breakfasts, the bus was soon on its merry way and Glen Etive was back on the cards. The hour was late, around 11.00am when the tents were erected near the Smiddy Hut at the head of Loch Etive. The skies were grey and foreboding and the forecast of strong winds and more blizzards to come in the afternoon really should have had the men staying tent-bound, but this was the NCR and there were mountains to be bagged. Some headed to Ben Starav and a couple went for Beinn Fhionnlaidh, while the trio of Frankie, Big Betty and Wee Ecky opted for Beinn Sgulaird. Given the lack of remaining daylight hours, the deep snow on the hills and the impending storms approaching, the plans were positively ludicrous, but to this group it was seen as a character-building adventure.

By early afternoon, the weather forecast was true to its word and with it brought a hellish wrath of fury and rage. This should have sounded the alarm bells, which it did for the Starav and Fhionnlaidh parties who descended in good order back to the tents. The Sgulaird trio, however, weighed up the situation while snow blasted their faces like pellets from a shotgun.

Frankie shouted his tuppence worth above the howling gale, 'This Beinn Sgulaird's stull aboot a hunder miles awa. How aboot we double back an' hammer up the Corbett o' Beinn Trilleachan so we dinna go back empty handed?'

'That's a great idea,' agreed Wee Ecky and off they went, heads down, trudging doggedly upwards into a white hell, all the while being buffeted, thrashed and challenged by an angry Mother Nature. This was all a mere stroll though, compared to what was waiting on the exposed summit ridge. Any markings or rock features were now obliterated in the white-out and navigating was down to taking a compass bearing and throwing a snowball on the right line on which to follow. This continued for some time as the ridge got narrower, with the fear of getting it wrong heightened in the knowledge that the famous 'Trilleachan Slabs' dropped sharply to the east and any mistake over a cornice would lead to certain death. A collective sensible decision called for a retreat and with very careful navigating, they eventually descended with the snow once again turning to rain just before darkness. Their return was met with great relief from their worried comrades.

Someone was kind enough to stay teetotal and offered their services to taxi the mob up to the Kingshouse Hotel where the old legendary climber's bar accommodated the rabble for a night of brotherly shenanigans. At closing time, they boarded the minibus in a disorganised conga of inebriated circus clowns, one numpty even appearing with a plug-in radiator which he said would 'heat his tent up'. This was duly confiscated from his clutches and returned to the hotel lobby as others argued that they didn't have an extension lead long enough to reach Loch Etive. The Corries' offering of 'Dark Lochnagar' rang out down the glen as the cat's chorus joined the flat singers and those who were way out of time in a woeful rendition which would have had Ronnie Browne and Roy Williamson cringing.

The folk singing soon came to an abrupt and sudden halt when allegations were made by those in the front that a rare Scottish wildcat had just run across the headlight beams and onto the hillside. Johnny V Diff rose up against popular opinion to proclaim, 'Yir ah talkin' shite! A wildcat meh erse! That wiz a mountain hare.'

'Awa an' dinna haver baloney. Your hade's fuhl o' mince V Diff. That wiz a WILDCAT!' replied the wildlife experts.

'It wiz nae bigger than a bothy cat ya drunken balloons,' fired back Johnny.

And so it went, all the way down the remainder of the glen until the minibus drew to a halt outside the Smiddy Hut, where lights were still on and a buzz of activity and laughter could be heard from within. The smell of smoke from a cosy fire tinged the nostrils of the jealous party assembled outwith and a few desperadoes suggested a bit of door-chapping and gate-crashing. The chilly, stiffening breeze had already encouraged a couple of the party to seek shelter in the nearby tents and slowly and rather reluctantly, the rest followed suit.

It didn't take long for the alcohol to do what alcohol does best and send the campers into a deep and contented slumber, the various tones and rhythms of snoring dancing hand-in-hand through the melody of encircling wind and complementing in a strange kind of way, the serenity and tranquillity of this most beautiful of settings. The surrounding mountain giants looked down almost sympathetically on the peaceful scene but gave no warning of what was coming.

The distant rumble began near the foot of the western flank of Ben Cruachan, much like the far off volleys of cannon fire that were exchanged by Wellington and Napoleon's opposing armies at the Battle of Waterloo. This rumble quickly gathered momentum, then turned into a deafening roar as it raced northwards, the length of Loch Etive. The impact of this freak gale was sudden and violent and it hit with such ferocity that some of the men woke up thinking their tents were about to be lifted straight off the ground. Seconds later, those who were awoken recalled a sinister and eerie phenomenon which sounded like people's voices circling round and round their tents. Indistinct words, but very much like cold whispers only inches from their ears.

Then it died and all was utterly calm. A short passage of time led to a false sense of security before the faint rumble began once more, then again and again in a seemingly never-ending cycle of hell. Someone commented that it felt like having your tent pitched on the runway at Heathrow airport and hearing the approaching thunder of a jumbo jet pass right over your nose. Men were literally spreading themselves across the four corners of the tents as each vicious blast shook and strained the small shelters to their absolute core. But it was the 'whispering voices' then the stone dead silence which followed each onslaught that had grown men curled tightly under their sleeping bags and genuinely gripped with bouts of overwhelming fear.

Wee Ecky, who was pitched in between the Bonnie Prince and Big Betty, whispered through the tent wall during a lull in the chaos, 'Betty, are you awake?'

'Fuckin' right eh am,' came the equally whispered reply. 'This is totally horrendous. Eh keep hearin' voices goin' roond ma tent.'

'Ehm the same, it's freakin' is oot.'

That night was to be one of the longest and most mentally enduring nights for each of the aforementioned men and not one of them would be considered soft or easily scared in any way. Something or someone had spooked them beyond their own normal reasoning. Yes, they'd had a good skinful of drink and yes they knew it was to get stormy through the night, but the strange and bizarre manner in which the cycle of events unfolded didn't make sense to them. At various points, they'd get up individually and walk around the tents to reassure themselves there was nothing untoward, only to get back into their sleeping bags and the spine-chilling feeling would begin again. Wee Ecky said at one point, he felt as though someone was kneeling on his chest and he couldn't shout or scream as he was paralysed with fear. It wasn't until daylight finally broke the next morning and the Bonnie Prince, Big Betty and Wee Ecky all shared very similar and uncanny experiences of their own personal nightmares. Amazingly, the others had either been spared from enduring the haunting rituals or were, in fact, too inebriated to appreciate the inferno of hell which was rampant around them.

It maybe wasn't coincidence either that the loch is associated with a Gaelic goddess with the name Etive, believed to translate into 'little fierce one' or 'little ugly one'. Something had definitely upset her that night and this may explain why she unleashed her full wrath on the glen.

A few months after that particular meet, Big Betty was reading through the latest edition of the *Scots Magazine* when a featured piece on Glen Etive covered stories from past centuries, revealing murder and mayhem and ghostly sightings. This could be true of most Scottish glens, but it did temporarily make his blood run cold.

Cammy and Wee Ecky were each nearing the end of their respective Munro journeys and with a prolonged period of settled and excellent weather upon them, they had taken a week off work from the daily drudgery of the factory and headed north and west on a bagging spree to tidy up some of the farthest and remotest summits.

They left Dundee very early on the Monday morning and climbed Sgùrr Ghairich in scorching sunshine before travelling to Kinloch Hourn and walking into Barrisdale bothy. Tuesday was another early start, climbing through the misty corries before reaching the summit of Ladhar Bheinn, once again in blazing sunshine. They returned to the bothy for the long walk back out and stayed in the proper bunkhouse at the Tomdoun Hotel (not the shitehouse mentioned in a previous chapter) and got in tow with a few locals and fishermen, which inevitably turned into a bit of a drunken session. It was a fairly groggy but determined effort to conquer Spidean Mialach and Gleadhraich next morning, then onto Sgùrr a' Mhorair in the afternoon, followed by a drive around to Glenelg, where tents were pitched on the beach and the nearby pub encouraged another session.

On Thursday, they were up at the crack of dawn and spoiled with another glorious burst of warm sunshine. They reached the summit of Beinn Sgritheal overlooking the dead calm and picturesque Loch Hourn at 9.00am, then proceeded to have a celebratory fry-up and a brew. Once down, the tents were packed and they were on their merry way to Kyle of Lochalsh for a fish supper, then it was north west to the little village of Achintee before the arduous six mile trek into Bearnais bothy, which lies in a real remote and lonely part of the country. This small abode has an entry porch that opens into a single room where the pair hoped to have a settled and comfortable night in preparation for the next morning's climb over Bidein a' Choire Sheasgaich and Lurg Mhòr. Given the exertions of a long, hard day, they had opted to bring no coal or wood, so there was to be no entertainment from the 'bothy TV' (fire). With a quarter bottle of whisky each and no one else in, they would have to make do with each other's company. Candles were lit to brighten the room up and bring some ambience and character.

Wee Ecky took a sip from a healthy-sized dram and began flicking through the pages of the bothy book. (Many bothies have these where attendees or those just passing through can leave a wee entry from their trip.) Cammy noticed his companion had gone quiet and had put down his dram.

'What's up?' he asked.

'Tak a look at this,' replied the wee man.

They both fixed their eyes on the latest entries, which contained strange references to Lucifer and rituals of walking anti-clockwise, three times around the bothy. A séance had been held and included a drawing of a pentangle, the widely recognised sign from bygone folklore to ward off evil spirits. After a few moments, the book was cast off across the table and verified as a 'load o' aald bollocks' before the men turned their attentions once more to the glasses of golden uisge beatha. Shortly afterwards, they both heard the familiar sound of footsteps approaching and thought 'Great, wull hae some company fir the night.' They waited for the door to open, but nothing happened. Looking at each other and somewhat confused, they shook their heads and went outside to have a look, but there was no one. They walked right around the bothy but found no sign of anyone or any wildlife. (For those who know Bearnais, it is situated in a very desolate, flat, and featureless area with no trees or certainly not when this trip was made, many years ago.)

They returned inside and thought that their minds must be playing tricks on them. Once again, they heard footsteps, but this time with sounds of knocking on the door and windows. Cammy said, 'Somebody's at the bloody capers oot there,' so they both leapt up, threw open the door and shouted challenges to whoever was out there. Again, nobody. They got back inside and agreed it had been a long and tough week and maybe they were just tired, so they fired up a brew and tried not to get too uptight, but they both said they felt a very eerie atmosphere around the place. The noises continued outside with strange scratching sounds on the walls, which could have been argued were deer scraping their antlers, if only there were any deer about.

By now, the men were extremely spooked and decided to turn in early, especially when a candle on the table had inexplicably gone out without any breeze or burning itself out. It was only 9.00pm, but they crawled into their sleeping bags and snuggled close together for security, both frightened to even move. It proved to be a very long and mostly sleepless night with bouts of scratching heard on the inner walls so they arose at 5.00am, had a very hurried breakfast, then grabbed their rucksacks and made off for the two Munros, trying desperately to make some sense of the night's eerie goings-on. Back at the bothy they made the quickest pack-up on record and beat a very hasty retreat to Achintee, never once looking back.

Some years later, the club returned to Bearnais following an epic march in winter with full weekend packs over the five Munros of Mòruisg, Sgùrr nan Ceannaichean, Maoile Lunndaidh, Sgùrr Chòinnich and Sgùrr a' Chaorachain with Lurg Mhòr and 'Cheesecake' falling on the Sunday. The only spirits encountered, however, on that particular meet were of the 40 proof liquid variety.

CHAPTER 12

Hold the Line

The full pack

SERIOUS CLIMBING WITH ropes and jangly bits and holding onto tiny notches with fingernails and toes (or ice-axes and crampons) while staring down at a gaping drop below isn't for everyone. It takes a special type of character to deal with heights and block out the natural instinct of the fear of falling. One must possess a strong, focused mind, a super high level of concentration and determination, the ability to route find and skilfully work out problems, be brave and totally committed, but above all else, they must have a fair degree of insanity. Humans evolved over many thousands of years to come down from the trees and walk upright on land and that is where the vast majority of the population of this planet is most happy.

But then there are some, whether it be through deep-held genetic links, who wish to climb, but not just climb. They look to challenge themselves to extreme levels and what certain individuals have achieved throughout the era of modern history is nothing short of miraculous.

As we heard earlier, various NCR club members were already involved in some climbing in the 1950s, with club President Frank Anderson leading the way pre-war. It was probably during the 1970s and into the 80s when a younger, more ambitious group emerged, some of whose fathers had taken them out as young laddies and showed them the ropes, so to speak. Others who followed learned from their experience, knowledge and guidance and pretty soon both summer and winter routes of various difficulties were being tackled.

Bruce had served a very early climbing apprenticeship with his dad and had steadily progressed onto more challenging routes with various club members over the years, but he formed a formidable partnership with his good friend Mikey Fitz. By their own admission, they were never top-end climbers and happy sticking to VS (Very Severe) or HVS (Hard Very Severe) in summer and Grade II to III in winter. They were well-travelled, tackling routes all over Scotland and the Islands, then further afield to Bulgaria, the Atlas Mountains, the Pyrenees, Yosemite and the Sierra Nevada range in western USA. It was during a climbing holiday to the latter that they both nearly came a cropper.

They had spent a long day on a multi-pitch route, but didn't fancy the long walk off to descend, so they found an alternative line of bolts on which they could abseil. Having never been on this particular route, this 'great idea' was literally a drop into the unknown. The first two abseils went without any problems. The third, however, was a whole different story. Bruce was lowering himself down, searching for the next belay station or bolt, acutely aware that he was coming to the end of the ropes. He dropped over a huge overhang and could see the ropes dangling freely in mid-air. The situation was desperate. He spotted a bolt on the underside of the roof and managed to swing himself in, clip onto it and mercifully, it held. He was safe but knew only too well that this old Californian bolt had seen many seasons and been battered by all kinds of weather and extremities.

He gave a loud shout and signalled Mikey to come down. Both

of them were now clipped into this old upside-down bolt and praying furiously that it didn't decide to leave the roof. With nerves shot to pieces, they somehow managed to sort the ropes, rig the next abseil from their single bolt and 150 ft later, they were down. They lay on the ground for the next ten minutes, acknowledging how wonderful it was to be alive before Bruce broke the silence and turned to his friend, 'Wut a pair o' stupid, lucky bastards. We'll no' dae that again!' They both burst into a nervous laugh and tipped their climbing helmets to Lady Luck.

A sustained and settled period of sub-zero conditions had enticed Bruce and some of the lads up to nearby Glen Clova for some winter climbing on the aptly named 'Winter Corrie' on Driesh. All of them were competent winter climbers and had chosen various Grade II routes on which to solo. The snow was solid with some steep ice bulges formed near the top of the corrie, providing excellent challenges and fun for the group. Bruce was having a great time and fancied spicing things up a wee bit, so ventured on to a particularly steep ice bulge where he made a stupid move and placed his right leg far too high. The result was, his crampon dislodged when he placed his weight on it and one of the front points sank straight into his left thigh. The air in the corrie turned bluer than the beautiful sky while Bruce fought desperately to free the foot from his punctured thigh. He momentarily contemplated just leaping off, but the landing was hundreds of feet below onto a nice bed of jaggy rocks.

The pain was excruciating as he took the gamble to unhook his right hand from the ice axe loop and somehow managed to pull his leg upwards and separate it from the other while hanging on with the left axe. Thankfully, the deep gash produced very little blood while a steady flow of adrenaline kept the pain bearable. Bruce finished his intended route along with the others and with much hobbling and wincing, he made it back to the corrie floor, where the lads administered some butterfly stitches and wrapped an old t-shirt around the wound. Back in Dundee, the wound was washed and new butterfly stitches were applied. There were no mobile phones available, no mountain rescue and the order of the day was self-rescue.

During the early 1980s, Bruce had been doing a lot of climbing with three good pals from Forfar who liked nothing better than travelling south, the dozen or so miles to Dundee and going right on the lash. Bruce's parents' house had become an unofficial bothy for dossing down following the mad nights spent painting the town red before heading up to Glen Clova the next day. The ground rules were, do not disturb the parents, do not enter Bruce's sister's room and remember to leave the latch off for the last man home. On one occasion, however, someone couldn't count and locked the door, leaving poor Tam out on a bitterly cold night. As it was 3.00am and mindful of the rules, the Forfar man simply crawled under the car in the driveway and went into the Land of Nod. It was breakfast time while Bruce's parents were rustling up the full Scottish fry-up when they noticed something odd under the car. It was, of course, a refrigerated Tam, slightly baltic and below functioning level. He soon thawed out though and, shortly afterwards, he was on his way with the rest and preparing for the challenge of the frozen Angus mountains.

Andy Ran Dan was one of the late '80s/early '90s members who had joined that magical era when the club was bolstered by a group of like-minded individuals looking for adrenaline on the mountains and also in the bars and bothies. As the name suggests, he did indeed enjoy *going on the Ran Dan*, (a Scottish term used loosely for having a wild time on the drink). Never one for huge hill days or ticking off Munros, he much preferred sampling craft ales and quaffing gin and tonic, way before they ever became *en vogue*. He was, however, involved in one monumental day when the club had based itself in Barrisdale bothy, way out west in Knoydart. The weather, as it is occasionally inclined to do, had turned hellish with rain battering the area for the whole day, but this didn't deter the baggers who set off for the thick misty summits of Luinne Bheinn and Meall Buidhe.

Ran Dan, Sweary Doug and Howzat Harvey had alternative plans and fancied a pint in the famous Old Forge in Inverie, the most remote pub on mainland Britain. With just over 9 miles on rough track and an ascent of over 2,000 ft over the Màm Barrisdale pass in biting, driving rain, it was going to prove a challenge. The return journey never even entered their minds, well, for now. The welcome from hosts Ian and Jackie Robertson was as warm and as welcoming as anywhere in the world where the craic flowed as freely as the beer. (The same cannot be said, however, for a certain individual who took over some years later, but that is a whole different story. He thankfully moved on and nowadays, the place is in the proud ownership of the community and thriving once more.)

Alas, when men get mixed up in great company and the old amber nectar is sliding down the throat steadily, all sensible thoughts get left at the door in favour of raucous laughter and talking shite. It was very late in the afternoon when the trio staggered out, half-canned onto the Inverie High Street and into the face of a monsoon onslaught. And just as poor Tam o' Shanter had found to his grave cost while returning on his horse 'Maggie' after a wild session in Burns' epic poem, dancin' wi' the Deil just wasn't funny any more. The three hardened mountaineers were soon greetin' like wee bairns as the enormity of the task ahead sank in like the rain sinking through their drookit clothes. The hour was late and darkness had set in long ago when the three drowned rats finally crawled into the bothy to be welcomed by a very relieved party of comrades who then proceeded to raise their glasses and propose a toast to 'the thirst of men and utter stupidity!'

Oh yes, climbing. At some point early on, Andy Ran Dan had sat down for a heart-to-heart chat with himself and questioned the path (or mountain track) he had been following thus far in life. The decision was made. There would be no more, or at least very little, plodding over mundane and featureless hills. Having enjoyed the hands-on scrambling on the Cuillins in Skye, he wanted some substance and meaning to his life, a buzz, an excitement, even danger, so he dived headlong, straight into the world of climbing. Under the watchful eye of some excellent climbing friends, namely Mackie and Broonie, he gradually gained the technique, experience and confidence to operate competently, firstly on rock and then onto snow and ice.

They honed their craft with frequent trips to Craig a Barns at Dunkeld, The Hawkcraig sea cliff, Binnein Shuas and Doug Lang's famous Ardverikie Wall (more about Doug later), Aberdeen sea cliffs, the Old Man of Stoer and many, many more. There was still the odd occasion when he found out the hard way that combining climbing with going on the Ran Dan wasn't a great idea. On a club weekender to the Isle of Arran, Andy and Neily had indulged heavily in knocking back tins of red wine all the way to Ardrossan, then hitting the pub there before the ferry. The result was total carnage and a long lie saw them sleep in till midday. With raging hangovers and both of them as green as the Incredible Hulk they made their way up onto Pagoda Ridge and were engulfed by 'the fear', compliments of last night's wild session. With nerves shot to pieces, they completed the route and agreed that the remainder of Saturday would be spent lying low, detoxing in the campsite. And yes, you could probably guess that a few hours later, they were right back in the mix with the rest, sampling the bright lights of Brodick and partying like there was no tomorrow.

With freezing temperatures and blue skies forecast, Ran Dan and Mackie had risen early to avoid the crowds and make a sharp start into the cliffs of Lochnagar. While still half-asleep and skirting round the side of Meikle Pap, they were passed at pace by two younger lads whose packs were hanging with gear. On arrival at their intended route, the spectacular Tough-Brown Traverse, they were gutted to find the two young lads had also chosen this and were preparing to climb. There was nothing for it; they would have to let them forge ahead. They followed the pair up the first pitch of the gully, then Mackie asked if Andy would like to lead the next pitch, which headed along a narrow shelf before going up again. He was well up for it and was edging his way carefully along the snowy ledge when he heard a commotion in the gully and saw a glove whizzing past Mackie, quickly followed by a twisted pile of ropes and a shouting, screaming climber who went tumbling down the slope. Moments later, his partner flew by in the same manner. Thankfully, they came to a halt and were seen moving while other climbers went rushing to their aid at the bottom.

Ran Dan remembered thinking that the omens didn't seem good, but the decision was made to press on. He took two steps along the snowy ledge when all hell broke loose and it collapsed, sending him flying off backwards. Mackie's alert reactions arrested the fall, which left Ran Dan hanging upside down and he was able to watch as Mackie's camera dropped out of his open pocket and went bouncing down the slope. Visibly shaken, he managed to compose himself, then climb back up to the belay, but the pair wisely decided to call it a day and descend. As they headed down, Ran Dan found a shiny new ice-axe which he secured onto his pack. They met with the two young lads, who were in shock, but apart from bruised limbs and pride, they were alive, having avoided hitting the many rocks scattered around. They explained what had happened and said they couldn't find any good belays so the lead climber had dug out a snow seat on which to secure his mate. This disintegrated when the second man slipped and off they both went. One of them asked if Andy or Mackie had dropped a camera and Andy, in turn, asked if they were missing an axe?

The exchange was made and they wished the two young lads well, just as an RAF Sea King helicopter thundered into the corrie, whereby the down-draught blew Andy Ran Dan's gloves off into obscurity. As they tramped back to the car park, they couldn't help but think how much climbing or experience the two young lads actually had. They'd certainly gotten away with one and arguably, so had the Dundee men.

It was a change of scenery and a slight change in climbing partners, which saw Ran Dan team up with the highly accomplished Brucie S, the ever-present Mackie and his mate Finn, who had tagged along for some excitement. The location was up the north east coast near Aberdeen and a cliff traverse route. With Brucie leading, they came to a 12 foot gap where he informed his comrades that they'd all have to jump into the sea to continue onto the next part. No problems and in they all went. Having completed the climb, they walked back to their gear and duly stripped off to change into dry clothes. The fact that they were standing naked near to a field full of sheep wasn't lost on them as a train sped by packed full of passengers. The men burst out laughing at the thought of conversations possibly going on in the carriages.

'Here Terence, it's true, it's true!' exclaimed Felicity, who had been busily knitting away when she happened to glance out of the window. She and her husband were on their very first holiday to

Scotland, having travelled up from Buckinghamshire.

'Yes darling, what is it?' answered Terence rather uninterested, his head still buried deep in his *Financial Times* newspaper.

'I've just seen a group of Aberdeen sheep-shaggers!'

Ran Dan was beavering away at his desk in the NCR when the phone rang. It was an internal call from Mackie asking if he fancied some ice-climbing on the magnificent frozen playground of the Coire Àrdair cliffs on Creag Mèagaidh. Conditions were reportedly good, so next morning they were up at 5.00am and sped off up the A9 heading for the Aberarder car park. They shouldered the heavy packs and began the march into Meagaidh, hindered frequently by the frozen railway sleepers on the path, which produced some award-winning pirouettes and face-plants. On reaching the small loch below the cliffs, Mackie suggested a cunning plan. 'If we walk straight ower the loch wull save aboot 20 minutes.'

Against his better judgement, Ran Dan agreed, thinking, 'Ach, he's musta done this afore.'

He gingerly followed in Mackie's footsteps, but around halfway, while staring at the mesmerising frozen tapestry of the corrie cliffs, he realised he had strayed away from his mate's footsteps. A few more steps forward, then 'CRACK', the ice broke and in he went. The shock of the cold water snatched his breath away, but luckily, he only went in waist-deep as the pack jammed on the icy rim. It was more than likely an air pocket which had collapsed under the weight and sensibly, Mackie stayed well clear so they didn't both end up in the freezing water. With some huffing and puffing and a determined effort, he managed to free himself and then made it safely to terra firma. After a brief discussion through chattering teeth and shivering, Ran Dan assured his mate that all was well and 'wir here now, so let's crack on'. He stripped off behind a large boulder, wrung his gear out as best he could, then put the freezing cold garments and boots back on.

Harnessed up and crampons on, they set off for their objective 'Centre Post Direct' graded v5 (which in layman's terms means 'quite mental'). Two climbers were already on it and, by all accounts, were taking ages and faffing around. Mackie, who was well aware of his friend's frozen predicament, grew ever more agitated until, accompanied by a cacophony of colourful expletives, he set off, climbing under the faffer's ropes to overtake them. The aforementioned pair had opted for the easier route, missing out on the vertical icefall. Mackie made it above the crux section and then shouted on Ran Dan to follow. Climbing as best he could, Andy was slightly alarmed to see water steadily trickling down the rockface behind the four or five inches of clear ice. On reaching the belay, he was then horrified to see a sling wrapped around a five inch column of ice with an ice screw as back-up further up. His nerves felt as though they were tiptoeing along a tightrope when Mackie said, 'Dinna kick the ice too hard, it's likely to go.'

And with those chilling words buzzing in his ears and all kinds of possible scenarios of 'what could have been' going round in his head, he followed his lead man up a snowy gully to the top before they both glissaded most of the way down Easy Gully. It certainly had been an eventful day.

With an invite to stay in the famous CIC (Charles Inglis Clark) Memorial Hut and experience 'The Ben' (Nevis) in full winter conditions, Ran Dan thought to himself, 'How kin eh refuse such an offer?' Built in 1928/29 by Dr and Mrs Inglis in memory of their son Charles, who was sadly killed in action during the First World War, it is situated in arguably one of the most dramatic settings in Scotland, below the north face of Ben Nevis. It's fair to say these inner walls could tell a million stories of past tales and derring-do, having housed countless characters from the ranks of climbing royalty.

The familiar pairing of Mackie and Ran Dan set off on a Friday evening with a fair amount of excitement in anticipation as to what lay ahead in this most prestigious of mountain huts. It was during the walk-in and weighed down with heavy packs that the latter realised, not being 'hill fit' wasn't a great idea. With a good breakfast and strong coffee in their bellies, they set off at 7.00am and after around 40 minutes of hard slog up snowy ground, they reached the foot of their intended climb – Zero Gully, graded v4.

As the hard breathing returned to normal, Mackie turned to his mate and asked, 'Wahrz the rope?'

The look on Ran Dan's face provided the answer before he even opened his mouth. 'Aw SHITE! Eh hung it on a peg in the hut last night an' forgot to pick it up.'

The air turned blue with a tirade of expletives ringing in Ran Dan's ears as he raced back down to fetch it. The mood was strained as the pair finally kitted up and set about the climb, Mackie leading and attacking the slope with a fiery determination. After only two pitches, he crashed his axe off a rock and broke one of the securing pins, rendering the blade useless. They swapped axes so he could carry on leading and belaying his mate. Ran Dan followed, floundering and flapping around with one good axe and the adze of the other, certainly not ideal on such a serious climb.

On one of the belay stances which he could barely stand on, Ran Dan noticed the rope tied onto an axe which was whacked into the hard-packed snow with an ice screw above it as back-up. Way down below, the rope got stuck on an icicle. From his very precarious position, he had to carefully untie the rope so it could be pulled through by Mackie, who once retrieved, then threw it back across the gully for Ran Dan to catch and re-tie on. This was all very unnerving to say the least, as the anchored axe was now slightly loose and didn't look very secure at all. Slowly, they progressed up some more pitches before reaching the long, multi-pitched snowbank above the ice, which they waded through in darkness and up onto the black summit plateau.

After eating what meagre snacks they had left, the pair worked their way round the cliffs in search of the long, steep Number 4 Gully where they could make their escape to the hut. They eventually located the stake with the number '4' drilled into it and prepared to descend. With a bite-shaped 'C' already out of the cornice from previous climbers' efforts, Ran Dan had a gaze into the abyss with his cheap head torch, but all he could see was a dark mass with no indication of where the slope started. In his shattered state, he thought it would be fine to just 'jump' into the gap, reckoning the slope would only be about 2 to 3 ft below. A little later, he would be very thankful as Mackie cautiously suggested they down climb just in case it was further than they thought. This call most certainly saved Andy Ran Dan's life as the first 15 ft were vertical!

Both men were absolutely knackered and out on their feet as

they carefully picked their way down before spotting the welcome beams of head torches far below in the glen. It was around 10.00pm when they entered the hut, where they were warmly greeted by a band of concerned fellow climbers who admitted they had feared the worst and were about to alert the rescue services. Exhausted and drained, both men gorged ravenously on all the food they had to regain some lost energy, but did triumphantly manage a couple of beers before collapsing in their bunks. (Shortly after this hair-raising episode, Ran Dan decided to hang up his ice-axes, fold away his rope and shelve his crampons. His climbing days were done.

Before he'd reached this final decision, however, Andy was very fortunate to have befriended the legendary Dundonian climber Dougie Lang and had even gone climbing with him on a few occasions. Although Dougie worked for NCR, he'd never joined the mountaineering club, much preferring the company of some of the most talented climbers of his generation and leaving in their wake a hugely impressive list of first ascents and seriously hard climbs all over Scotland. As well as the incredible trailblazing climbs, Dougie became President of the famous SMC (Scottish Mountaineering Club) from 1992–94. He sadly died in an avalanche in his beloved Corrie Fee in Glen Doll, a place which he held dear to his heart and in a cruel twist of fate, near to where his first pioneering winter ascent of B Gully Chimney had begun.

There was an uncanny connection to that fateful weekend 18 March 2011 as the NCR club were based in the nearby bothy of Glas Allt Shiel on the shores of Loch Muick. A huge deluge of fresh snow had fallen sometime on the Friday and had proven extremely challenging for all of the members who had attempted to go out on the hill the following day. Indeed, Big Geordie and Big Betty had gotten into some difficulty on a banked-out wall of deep snow near the Capel Mount Pass and were very grateful that it hadn't avalanched. It wasn't until they returned to Dundee on the Sunday and heard the terrible news that Dougie had been found not too far from where the club were themselves.

Ran Dan's personal memories of his time spent with Dougie were of his insatiable enthusiasm and drive, even for a man considered to be in his 'later years of life'. His kindness and willingness to share his knowledge, along with his warm smiles and companionship, were altogether truly infectious. Rather comically, he remembers Dougie on numerous occasions disappearing off behind a rock or a corner for a dump before starting a climb. Possibly pre-match nerves, even for a maestro! He related a hilarious story (although not at the time) to Ran Dan when he'd gone to climb the famous Matterhorn in the Alps. On the morning of the ascent, he'd been suffering from a serious dose of the shits and had gone to a local pharmacy to acquire some Imodium or the like, but somewhere in the conversation, the translation was lost and he ended up with tablets that make you shit non-stop. He howled with laughter as he recalled being 'very weak' during the climb. A proper legend in every sense of the word.

And finally, it was time for the novices. Having heard many of the climbing escapades from fellow members over the years, the newer breed of Munro Baggers during the 1990s began to talk amongst themselves and say, 'Eh, ehl hae some o' that as well.' Off they went to the local outdoor shops to purchase climbing harnesses, figure 8s, karabiners and specialised 'sticky' climbing shoes and with a backpack full of eagerness and excitement, they marched off with their friend and guide, Johnny V Diff, to the Craig a Barns crags just outside Dunkeld.

Adrenaline began to surge through the small assembled group as they listened intently to Johnny's instructions.

'Right, wull keep it simple, git warmed up on a wee Moderate then continue through a couple o V Diff's (Very Difficult).

To any non-climbers, a 'Moderate' equates to 'Shitin' yir breeks' then gradually progresses all the way up to 'Suicidal'. Everyone was fairly comfortable in the art of scrambling, so no ropes were produced as Johnny led up the first climb, the aptly named 'Hairy Gully', which some did find bordering on 'hairy'. The cliff was busy that fine sunny day and the NCR boys stared in wonderment as a couple of daredevils further along were soloing up some crazy-looking vertical routes. A few V Diff's (with ropes) were successfully tackled before the next challenge reared up, which was also a V Diff – 'Holly Tree Groove'.

The Bonnie Prince, Wee Ecky and Big Betty volunteered to have a go at this one and were mindful of Johnny's parting words as he roped up and led off. 'Now mind, if ya git inta difficulty jist shout 'tight rope' an' ehl secure ya. Yir safe wi' me an' no' goin' anywahr.'

They waited until Johnny was up and over and securely tied in before getting the signal for the first man to climb. Wee Ecky stepped up to the wall and began climbing, but wasn't ideally equipped with heavy, clumpy hill-walking boots on his feet. The initial 20 or 30 feet went well until he came to a large chockstone blocking the way. A fairly awkward move was required to reach around and advance, but given the wee man's lack of inches, this was proving increasingly problematic. He began to flap and flounder around, searching desperately for a hold, then started calling to Johnny for a tight rope, but V Diff couldn't hear him over the lip of the crag. Wee Ecky glanced fearfully down to his comrades for some moral support, but received none as they both struggled to hold their laughs in. Eventually, there was some movement on the rope, but Johnny had misheard and began serving some slack.

Wee Ecky was now in utter panic mode and clutching the rope with both hands while his boots slid and scraped on the rockface. The wee man was by now consumed with terror and shouting down to the Bonnie Prince and Big Betty to alert V Diff of his predicament. The pair were doubled over, crying with laughter as the rope slackened once more. Fellow climbers were also howling as they witnessed the scene, which was like something out of a *Carry On* film. The wee man was finally lowered down safely, visibly shaken and confidence shattered.

At length, Johnny appeared, unaware of the drama which had unfolded below and asked, 'How'd ya git on Ecky?'

'Ehl fuckin' how'd ya git on ya prick! Eh thought eh wiz gonna deh up there!'

The laughter erupted once more, but that, for the time being anyway, was the end of the interest in climbing with ropes and jangly bits for some.

Wee Ecky did return to climbing many years later and conquered a few of the Scottish classics, the most notable being a winter assault over the Aonach Eagach.

A' Chùil, A' Chùil, We Ah Fell Doon

The Sherpa express went Glendessary bound
But treh as they wid, A' Chùil couldna be found
Fumblin' aboot in the caald, starlit night
Sumdee piped up, 'thirz somethin' no' right'
The daydreamin' band somehow missed the wee hoose
An' kept headin' west tae chase a wild goose
Wi' a possible bivvy in the Highland expanse
Greig bugled the retreat, tae halt the advance

Mackie wuzna half gled when A' Chùil's silhouette
Appeared an' allowed him tae cease brewin' sweat
Nae wonder, wi' a pack cradlin' eighteen tins
An' no' the variety that held beans or mince
Sehturday saw the troops on hilltop manoeuvres
Gairich, Sgùrr na Cìche an' Sgùrr Mòr amongst ithers
The clan-less land now a playground fir sheep
Whar once voices sang an' traditions ran deep

By evenin' that wee hoose in 'Glen Solitude'
Had rekindled spirits o' the warrior brood
A ceilidh which the ancients woulda been proud
Now rattled the wa's, boisterous an' loud
Mackie, wa'd kerried in the massive kerry-oot
Wiz decked on three tins, while the rest fell aboot
A herculean hike on a ridge line Big Dipper
Had him weary an' searchin' fir a sleepin'-bag zipper

Now the Angel o' Alcohol flew in wi' a spell
An' summoned the hill men tae join her in Hell
The Dark an' Satanic pied-piper played her tunes
While the whisky brigade danced like malt-possessed loons
Greig, wah beh now wiz a mutterin' wreck
Swallyed doon anither an' said 'Wut the heck?'
Then he staggered ootside an' fell on the tree
An' decorated its branches wi' a hot vomit spree

Nae quaarter wiz given fae ringmaster or clown
The pished paparazzi said 'Smile' tae the downed
The Kodak congregation gave the big man the works
An' laughed the laugh o' wild-eyed Young Turks
Jist anither stretcher-case o' bothy survival
A regular competitor on the monthly revival
Alas, fire an' candle, burned oot thir last
An' the snorers snored an' the farters rasped

At the dawn o' the morn, Big Geordie awoke
Tae find on eez bag, a huge pile o' boke
He tried tae adopt a position that wid suit
But the internal pizza rolled inta Charlie's boot
The Bonnie Prince rose wi' a mountain in mind
But plans wir aborted when the baits he did find
'Ok, wut numpty filled up ma bait?'
Nae bugger answered, leavin' Charlie irate

An' so wiz born the curse o' A' Chùil
Whar the demon drink sank, the unwittin' fools
'A' Chùil, A' Chùil, we ah fell doon'
An' the boxer ca'd 'Whisky' danced ah aroond

This was indeed the club's first sortie into Glen Dessarry on the eastern edge of the Rough Bounds of Knoydart and a real mountain paradise full of rugged Munros and Corbetts. The area features a fantastic network of remote bothies which can be linked either for low-level treks or excellent bases for some of the harder-to-reach summits.

Mackie was just one of many who, over the years, was to realise the brutal reality and hardship of lugging a huge carry-out into a bothy. Then there were those who managed to drink the lot... and some. For those who remember the little Xmas tree outside the front door, this was where Greig was found hugging it desperately for all he was worth. Sadly, it's no longer there, no doubt another victim of the brainless bothy vandals who cut down live wood.

The jury was out on Big Geordie, who, to this day, is still being accused of directly filling the Bonnie Prince's boot with spew. His defence of it being dark and trying to move the pile safely off his sleeping bag has never been accepted.

This was just the first of many eventful visits to this cracking bothy, where the curse did indeed return, wholly aided and abetted by the demon drink.

CHAPTER 13

Big Flatters

Bearnais bothy

THERE HAS BEEN a fabulous array of uniquely wonderful and at times, chaotic characters who have graced the NCR club's long and colourful history, some briefly and some who made it their lives, or as far as their bodies could physically carry them. Big Flatters was one such man who deserves a few of these pages all to himself. Hailing from England's green and pleasant land, he had travelled north at some point, where he found work at the now-defunct Dounreay Nuclear Plant on the far north coast of Scotland. A highly educated and intelligent man, he transported his skills to the burgeoning NCR business during the 1980s. Having no accommodation secured (he was indeed a spectacularly thrifty man), he spent around six months camping in the nearby Camperdown Park, which took him through an extremely harsh and freezing winter, but this hardship was mere child's play to a man whom fellow members would soon find out about.

BIG FLATTERS

With an unquenchable passion for fitness and the outdoors, this powerhouse soon joined the mountaineering club, hardly missing a day or weekend meet, such was his appetite for the mountains. With a pair of thighs like a power lifter, he soon began demolishing the list of Munros for fun. He was very much a loner who liked to operate mostly solo, often jumping off the minibus early and disappearing into the night to go and doss down in some dilapidated shack or hovel. As a member of the Dundee Hawkhill Harriers running club and a seasoned long-distance runner who often partook in 24-hour ultramarathons, it was no wonder no one could keep up with him, although he did also enjoy the company of the group on a good few occasions. It is no insult to say he was hugely eccentric and not much of a drinker and often the rough and ready working class banter and hard bevvying would seem very alien to him, but the lovable giant fitted in with the motley crew just perfect, or nearly anyway.

It is told, by some of those who sat next to him on the minibus, that, owing to his massive enthusiasm for the mountains, he would begin a story in Perth and still be telling it by the time they reached Inverness. Big F wasn't really known for his dulcet tones or being a top crooner by any stretch of the imagination, but on the rare occasions where he strayed over his limit of two pints, he could be persuaded to get up and sing. Now I use the word 'sing' in the kindest of terms, as anyone who was unlucky enough to have heard his live performance would agree, he wasn't the best. If truth be told, he was positively awful, but it's all about the taking part.

One night in The Old Forge in Inverie, two guys were providing the night's musical entertainment and by all accounts were utterly horrendous.

The call went out somewhat jokingly, 'Mon Flatters, you kin dae better than that shite, git up there an dae a wee turn.'

Not expecting the big Englishman to step up, the group were left speechless when he took the mic and proceeded to wade his way through what seemed like 85 verses of his own personal favourite, 'The Wild Colonial Boy' and all eloquently delivered in a dire, non-melodic, monotone dirge. It is said that by the time he reached the final line of the song, tumbleweed was rolling through the deserted bar on a shrill whistling wind. Most of the patrons had either run off into the hills to take their chances with the packs of marauding wolves or dived into the black waters of Loch Nevis. Even the two shite musicians were seen sinking in the depths, having abandoned their instruments at their post.

Out of the bars, however, it was the mountains where the big man excelled and the wilder and more challenging the conditions, the better. Some of his escapades became the stuff of club legend. One baltic October morning, having spent a freezing night camped in Glen Shiel, the majority of the group packed up and made their way onto the eastern end of the snow-plastered South Glen Shiel Ridge to take in the seven Munros, then camp at Loch Duich near the Kintail Lodge Hotel. Trudging through knee-deep snow and in worsening conditions, the large group battled on, everyone to a man fully clad in Gore-Tex suits of armour, wearing all additional items of warm clothing they possessed.

Around three quarters of the way along, a figure was spotted through the thickening flurries of snow, heading in the opposite direction. It was Big F who was decked out in a battered old wafer-thin cagoule, a pair of ancient rubber binman's gloves and outrageously, a pair of shorts. His friends nearly fell off the ridge in astonishment. After swapping a few pleasantries, he was off into the blizzard and away to his happy place.

He'd completed his round of the Munros in no time (or so he thought), but one day, whilst browsing through his diary of climbs, he found to his horror that he'd actually missed Ben Lomond. Without any hesitation, he set out at the crack of dawn the next morning, pedalled all the way to the Trossachs, climbed the rogue summit, then pedalled all the way home again.

When it came to material items or possessions, Big Flatters was as anti-conforming as he could possibly be, much preferring the simple, basic things in life. As was described earlier, his gear was completely spartan and he generally refused to use cosmetic products such as soap or deodorant, which caused a few contentious issues, especially in the factory, where he was reported on more than one occasion for his lack of personal hygiene. This didn't phase the big man at all as he was completely set in his ways. This point was proved when the club had spent a fine winter weekend up in Glencoe and following a huge day in the hills on Saturday, the big man decided to join the group for a Sunday climb up the impressive snow-covered Sgùrr na h-Ulaidh.

The scorching sunshine had everyone down to their base layers, including Big F, who was wearing his faithful old bri nylon shirt from the 1920s. The descent was taken at a pace as each man flew down the deep, powdery snow. Flatters unfortunately went arse over tit and narrowly escaped serious injury when his ice-axe tore through his prized vintage shirt. Incredibly, this same shirt was still on his back on Monday and no doubt another deluge of complaints from his fellow office workers as they may have battled through swarms of flies.

The club took part in a few charity fundraising events and one of these saw a large group take on a 50-mile weekend hike beginning at Tomintoul, then snaking through the Cairngorms before finishing at Blair Atholl. Some men's bodies and feet were in bits as they gathered in a bar to celebrate with a well-earned pint or three. It was then that someone piped up, 'Wut the hell is that god-awful reek? It smells like a decomposin' carcass!'

The answer soon became apparent when Big Flatters' tattered trainers and socks were found discarded under the table to reveal two feet which had botanical gardens of fungus growing on them. The stench was stripping the wallpaper off the walls.

He didn't confine his walking and climbing to the British Isles and had a few epic adventures on foreign soil with the Faroe Islands, Lapland, Norway and France among them. As always, he'd chosen the bargain basement budget options, travelling as cheaply and independently as possible. It was alleged, but with a fair degree of confirmation, that his supplies for his assault on Mont Blanc consisted of a bag o' tatties (potatoes). The trip nearly ended in disaster when he became frostbitten after losing the location of his pitched tent and had to sleep out in a bivvy bag.

Fred was talking with him in the work prior to his trip to Norway and politely asked if Big F would be treating himself to a bus or train journey to catch the ferry in Aberdeen? As tight as ever, the answer was totally predictable as he pedalled the 70 or so miles with a pack the size of a caravan on his back.

His epic trip to Lapland was also done on a shoestring budget but nearly came back to haunt him with poor planning and a serious underestimating of the harsh and unforgiving environment. During the three weeks, there were many days when he was properly out in the middle of nowhere, covering hard miles in snow and only managing to pick up supplies sporadically in little stores. His famed thriftiness meant travelling as light as possible and supplementing his diet by living off the land, catching the odd fish or delving into some reindeer carcass (or any other carcass for that matter). On his final few days, the hardships caught up with him and with no supplies, exhausted and starving, he had to leave his tent and march some 30 miles to the nearest village to pick up some food, then return to collect his gear. As shattered as he was, it was a monumental effort which would have finished all but the toughest of characters.

Now, roadkill isn't most (if any) people's idea of a wholesome meal, but to Big Flatters this was exquisite cuisine and much more to the point, it was free. What state it was in, having been rattled from a car or lorry, mattered little. How fresh was it? Who could tell but the big man was a connoisseur of the furry and feathered roadside menu. Many a time he'd be out for a cycle, then suddenly leap off his bike to bag a dead rabbit or pheasant or such like. There were even reports of small deer making it back to his fridge. Then, on the odd occasion, on a weekender, he'd return to the minibus on the Sunday with some animal or bird stuffed in his pack, which went down really well with the others.

I did say earlier he was rather eccentric and with eccentricity comes behaviour some would often view as bizarre or mental. The Big F had got himself into the much-loved but seldom practised art of taxidermy. Self-taught and self-financed, his creations by all accounts were never going to adorn the display cabinets of Buckingham Palace or Balmoral Castle and would be much more at home in Dr Frankenstein's laboratory. Johnny V Diff it was, who many years ago was invited to the fabled House of Flatters for a birthday bash and was introduced to some of the big man's handiwork. V Diff told of seeing species which had never walked this planet but were proudly on show, mounted for all to admire. There was a stoat with three eyes and one ear, which had the torso of a capercaillie and also a creature which looked like a badger but had six legs and the tail of a fox. I am, of course, using a bit of poetic licence, but V Diff did admit there were some belters in the collection.

Tragically, the big man was killed in an accident in 1996 whilst cycling home from work. It was a huge loss for both his family and everyone who was lucky enough to call him a friend. He was many things: tough, driven, inspiring, kind and friendly, but above all, he was a gentleman. In what was a huge gesture of kindness from his family, a large part of his estate was donated to the building of the new Glencoe Mountain Rescue Centre situated in the village itself.

It was fitting then that the magnificent Pap Of Glencoe mountain was chosen as the summit on which to scatter his ashes and along with his family, a full coachload of club members attended while Big Betty played a lament on the pipes. In a scene which surely would have had the big man laughing, each person, when instructed, threw their handful of ash and said their own personal goodbyes. The Bonnie Prince commented that he was sure he'd got one of Big F's feet as the moment he launched it, a gust of wind blew it back in his face.

The send-off in the Clachaig Bar was complete mayhem as stories were shared through both tears of sadness and volleys of howling laughter. He was gone but certainly never forgotten.

CHAPTER 14

The Highland Hullabaloo

Suardalan bothy

MANY YEARS AGO, in an age before the likes of the Cape Wrath Trail and the TGO Challenge had gained widespread popularity, bringing at times large numbers into some of the most remote parts of Scotland, a walk of epic proportions was self-planned through a section of some of the wildest and most rugged terrain in the Highlands. The club was no stranger to huge treks in the mountains, but this was to be a sustained walk over eight gruelling days with an air of uncertainty as to whether the group could actually complete it. Maps had been studied then re-studied with goals set for each leg, which is all fine when looking at pieces of paper in the comfort of one's home, but the real challenge would come with how well the bodies could cope, not to mention weather conditions, river crossings and having enough rations.

Wee Ecky, Johnny V Diff, the bold Sir Lancelot, Ronnie Mac and newcomer Annie T were dropped off at Dundonnell in the north west of Scotland and said their goodbyes to Big Geordie, then shouldered their massive packs before setting off for the stiff uphill march into Shenavall bothy. The mood was one of excited anticipation as to what lay ahead for them.

A fair morning dawned for what was to be a long, long day heading for a B&B at Cromasaig, south of Kinlochewe. Following a couple of big river crossings, they stopped briefly at Carnmore bothy under the towering western crags of majestic A' Mhaighdean for a much-needed feed, then it was up and over the high pass of Bealach Mheinnidh and down to Letterewe on the shores of beautiful Loch Maree. By the time they reached the B&B they were long overdue and the highly concerned owner had been out looking for them for ages. Each person was shattered, with Annie T in particular already toiling. They were all very grateful for the huge meal and the comfy beds awaiting their drained bodies.

In lashing rain, they set off early next morning, heading south, passing through the Coulin Forest before arriving at Achnashellach Station. It was here that nearly all of the group were suffering from blistered feet and a huge dose of motivation and determination was needed firstly, to safely cross the wide and flowing River Carron, then the arduous pull up and over the high pass before the long descent to Bearnais bothy. On arrival, they were greeted with a warm welcome from Fred Mac, who had travelled up to surprise them and with a bottle of malt in his pack, he was ready to party. Unfortunately, his comrades were completely knackered and the big man had to be content with getting pished and talking to himself all night.

After saying cheerio to Fred, the group set off on what was to be their shortest but still a tough day, contouring around Beinn Dronaig to one of the most remote bothies in the country – Maol Bhuidhe. Here they were able to rest and tend to blistered feet, but the bold Sir Lancelot forfeited his downtime and opted to play with a candle instead. This didn't end too well as he gave himself a nasty burn, but his piercing screams received no sympathy and were met only with laughter from his audience.

Tuesday morning, they awoke to the raging symphony of torrential rain battering the bothy windows and this continued all day as they drearily trudged past Iron Lodge and on to Carnach before making the steep climb over a pass. Taking a southerly bearing, they entered a lonely glen which offered no respite from the hellish conditions, cursing blind as they waded through four miles of what felt like never-ending bogs. Spirits lifted ever so slightly as they eventually reached the path which would take them east to the sanctuary of Alltbeithe Youth Hostel and a cosy fire.

Wednesday began where Tuesday had left off, absolutely chucking it down. The mood was rock-bottom as the small group passed under the giants of Ciste Dhubh, Beinn Fhada and the Five Sisters, but hopes were high at the prospect of reaching the Kintail Lodge Hotel for a piping hot meal and a couple of pints. Absolutely demoralised didn't even come close to describing their feelings when they saw the 'CLOSED' sign displayed on the door. A quick bite in the local garage didn't quite match expectations, but they were able to replenish dwindling food stocks. An air of utter dejection hung over the party as they headed back out into the driving rain before a long pull over yet another pass to reach Suardalan bothy. The place was manky inside with mouse droppings everywhere and outside, a small herd of cows ambled around on the lawn shitting at will. The water supply didn't look too cheery either, with the burn running a murky brown colour. Yes, home sweet home for the night with a large helping of misery for company.

And then a miracle happened. Thursday morning saw the bothy basking in a picture portrait, baked by warm rays of golden sunshine under a magnificent azure sky. A solitary jet left a white, fluffy trail across the bluest of backdrops while all around, birds sang harmoniously on the light summer breeze. Well, that's how the story might go in an ideal world, but this certainly wasn't the ideal world. As the bothy door swung open, each person was cut down by the machine-gun volleys of ferocious rain. They didn't stand a chance as the lashing fury stung their faces. If putting wet boots, socks and clothes back on earlier had felt uncomfortable and depressing, that was nothing to the nightmare day which lay ahead.

Even the smallest of streams raged in spate and a few deep river crossings had to be carefully negotiated before a long energy-sapping march over a bealach, then it was down to the little village of Arnisdale on the shores of Loch Hourn, where a small boat was waiting to ferry them over to Barrisdale. A westerly wind howled in from the Sound of Sleat, causing a rough swell on the open water. With no life jackets issued, it was one very relieved band of landlubbers who gratefully detached their grip from the boat and set foot on terra firma in the bay. The bothy gave welcome shelter as stoves were fired up and many a warm brew was sunk, but this was just a brief interlude.

Everyone to a man (and woman) admitted that the hardest decision of the whole week was to leave that remote haven, don the sodden gear once more, then step back out into the pishing rain and gales, climb the Màm Barrisdale and navigate the track down to Inverie – nine long miles of pain and suffering. Poor Annie T, who had never undertaken anything remotely as serious as this, was literally out on her feet and almost broken both physically and mentally. In fact, the whole group were faring no better, but with an iron will and a strong bond of companionship, they motivated each other to simply keep putting one foot in front of the other, then finally staggered into the Inverie bunkhouse like a bunch of extras from a zombie apocalypse movie.

Spirits lifted immensely and there was even a slight spring in the step as they walked the half mile to The Old Forge, where a food menu fit for champions and a fine selection of ales and spirits awaited. Johnny V Diff had never had monkfish before, so opted for that while the others ordered various other dishes which, when served up, never stood a chance with the ravenous hikers. After only a couple of pints, Annie T and V Diff were feeling the effects of a monumental day and decided to head back to the bunkhouse.

The trio of Ronnie Mac, Wee Ecky and the bold Sir Lancelot, however, had other ideas and, in keeping with the club traditions of the more boisterous factions, set right in about the malt whisky menu. They waded through this with the same commitment they had given to wading through the countless rivers and streams of the previous days, which predictably brought the desired effect – steaming drunk! All hardships, aches and pains were completely erased from frazzled minds as they tripped and stumbled back to their welcoming bunks.

During the very early hours of the morning, Wee Ecky was awakened in his top bunk after hearing someone shuffling around the room. Still half-canned, he grabbed his head torch and switched it on to see what the commotion was. Johnny V Diff was wandering about, somewhat distraught in his boxer shorts. Wee Ecky asked if he was OK and what the hell he was doing?

'Ecky, please dinna tell anybody. Ehv shat ma bag,' came the whispered reply.

Wee Ecky nearly fell out of his bunk laughing. He ended up holding onto the bedposts in absolute hysterics while his stricken friend paced around, whimpering, trying desperately to keep his arse cheeks clamped tightly together. The whole group was now awake, including a stranger, and the room quickly filled with uproarious laughter as poor Johnny tried his best to clean the sleeping bag. He was, in fact, really ill and no sooner had he left the toilet, he was straight back in again on numerous occasions. Whether it was the monkfish, the filth at Suardalan of mouse-droppings, piss and a dirty water supply or simply, just a slack sphincter, no one knows. One thing was certain: there was no way he could finish the final two days of the trek and needed to get home pronto. The only problem was, pronto is not a word that is associated with the remotest community on mainland Britain. He probably had a better chance of getting to Dundee quicker from the moon.

When the laughter had finally died down, there was a genuine air of sadness and despondency as the rest of the group said their goodbyes to Johnny before heading on the long march through Gleann Meadail, up and over the huge Màm Meadail pass, then down to Sourlies bothy. A much-hoped-for tranquil and peaceful night's sleep was obliterated by a stranger who was snoring like a hippo with laryngitis. It is said he was extremely lucky not to have ended up having a permanent sleep in the nearby ancient graveyard of Eilean Tioram!

In typical fashion, the sun decided to put in an appearance for the final leg of the journey, the long tramp out through Glen Dessarry, where Big Geordie was waiting to greet them at Strathan. They reached their destination exhausted with bodies completely shredded, but the small band of comrades were rightfully elated at having achieved one helluva challenge. On summing up, they all agreed it had been brutal and much tougher than anticipated, with unforgiving terrain, grinding ascents and at times almost biblically harsh weather, but their characters had most definitely gained a new layer of armour.

Johnny V Diff's retreat from Inverie was up there with Napoleon's retreat from Moscow during the ill-fated campaign of 1812 and possibly eclipsed it owing to the fact that the famous French Emperor had not had to deal with following through in his sleeping bag.

Annie T had tried desperately to encourage V Diff to carry on with them and made the valid suggestion of 'just turning his bag inside out'. He politely declined her offer and explained that the bag looked like it had been dipped in a huge tin of oxtail soup.

After saying cheerio to his friends, he had boarded the 8.00am ferry to Mallaig and instantly felt even more nauseous and sickly as the boat bobbed and dived in the sea swell. At the local tourist information office, he was informed that the train to Fort William had already left and the next bus wasn't leaving for another four hours. There was no alternative but to start walking and stick out a thumb in the hope that some kind driver would pick up a lone hitch-hiker. Shortly afterwards, a young couple stopped and V Diff gratefully accepted a lift. Being in the hills for a week and wearing the same clothes, he admitted that he must have been completely stinking, not to mention the large mishap, which was conveniently omitted from any conversations. The lowered windows in the car were a dead giveaway that fresh air was scarce and the poor couple must have been mighty relieved to offload their cargo of human dung.

The only available option Johnny had from Fort William was a bus to Stirling, then a bus to Perth and finally a bus from there to Dundee. It was a grand total of 13 and a half horrendous hours over land and sea before he was met by his wife, who duly took him to the nearest farm and had him rinsed in the sheep-dip.

CHAPTER 15

The Quick Way Down

Blackburn bothy

THERE IS NO escaping the fact that climbing mountains can be dangerous. The simple trip, stumble or slip can prove disastrous and, sadly, for some, fatal. For the individuals on the outside who are not familiar with the art of mountaineering, it is all too easy to pass judgment on something they know very little of or nothing about. In truth, no one sets out to deliberately fall off a mountain or get buried in an avalanche, but the very nature of the game dictates that danger exists in varying degrees, especially in winter. Unfortunately, for some club members (and totally against their will), they have succumbed to gravity's pull and taken the 'quick way down the mountain'.

The powerfully fit and life-loving Davie San seemed to have the lion's share when it came to mishaps, although some were self-inflicted, as was documented earlier in the burning sleeping bag incident. In another disastrous episode (though not a fall),

THE QUICK WAY DOWN

he'd scaled Ben Macdui one late Springtime in glorious sunshine. The unexpectedly seasonally warm weather had persuaded him to don shorts and when he reached the summit around midday, he decided to have a little nap. Some three hours later, he was stirred from his slumber by a passing cross-country skier who was a little concerned for his welfare. The scorching sun had turned his legs scarlet, bringing burning agony and severe sunstroke. As hard and tough as he was in the hills, he would later admit that the long walk back to camp at Linn o' Dee was sheer hell. Still, he made it to the old bar at Mar Lodge where the others were holding court. They gave him no quarter as he was rounded on and ripped mercilessly.

Another eventful situation which found its way into Davie's catalogue of mishaps came when he had taken his 12-year-old son a meet to Laggan and went out to climb Creag Mèagaidh. They reached the summit plateau in rapidly worsening conditions, which then became a full-blown white-out. Disoriented and hugely aware of the nearby precipitous Coire Àrdair cliffs, Davie made the decision to dig a makeshift snow-hole and shelter them both. The weather by now was horrendous. Fellow club members were worried when the pair hadn't returned and had gone into the corrie to see if they could spot any torchlight. The Mountain Rescue were called at 8.00pm and as there was a youngster involved, they bravely went out into the fury of the storm to try and locate them.

Around midnight, the radio crackled into life with the message that the search dog was onto a scent, but try as they might, they could not find the father and son and had to call off the search till morning. At first light, Davie and his son departed the snowy tomb, which most certainly had saved their lives and there, only 20 yards away, were the multiple footprints left by the Rescue Team from the previous night. Though it was misty, the wind had dropped considerably and they were able to make out features to safely begin descending. Shortly afterwards, a helicopter spotted them and picked them up and while the pair were both frozen, hungry and exhausted... they were alive.

Davie's crowning glory of mishaps came not on some jagged, exposed ridge or vertical rock face but on some rather insignificant little mound, once more in the Laggan area. Most of the lads had left early morning on their own climbs, so Davie went for a canny dander to the little summit of Creag Ruadh, which has a monument on it, visible from the A86 road. Whether this 'canny dander' involved a detour to the Monadhliath Hotel for a few light refreshments beforehand, no one knows. He'd somehow managed to fall off the crags beside the monument and break his leg, but as none of the others knew where he'd gone and with the invention of mobile phones still many years away, he had to crawl agonisingly down the steep and rough hillside.

A passing car picked him up and once back at camp, Duncan and Bruce took him up to Raigmore Hospital in Inverness, where he was kept in to have his leg pinned and patched up. On the return to Laggan, they hit a deer, which caused some considerable damage to the minibus, while the poor beast bolted into the darkness. Three days later, they travelled back up to Inverness to collect the plaster-cast Davie and the following night, they were gathered in a pub in Dundee purely for medicinal purposes and tactical discussions on how soon he could get back on the hill.

On a beautiful winter's day, high on the spectacular Central Gully of Ben Lui a group of club members were carefully kicking steps into the semi-hardened snow and driving axes in deep when all of a sudden, Nick stumbled then flew off down the mountain, tumbling and careering over a few large buttresses while his friends watched in utter horror. Big Flatters reacted in an instant and, without any thoughts for his own safety, went bounding and leaping straight down the slope after his friend. Nick had fallen around 400 ft and although battered and bruised, he was able to hobble back down with the aid of a few others while Big Flatters hammered back up the gully and continued over the four Munros. And in the time-honoured tradition of the club, Nick was taken into the pub in Tyndrum to lick his wounds and numb the pain with a full night of bevvying.

As one half of the infamous Dangerous Brothers, Big Geordie was indeed no stranger to danger and positively thrived on challenging situations when the adrenaline began to flow. However, he came a cropper following a fine day spent on a snow-plastered Creag Mèagaidh. He was in the company of Broonie and Mackie,

THE QUICK WAY DOWN

who could easily have joined the ranks of the Dangerous Brothers themselves and both were excellent summer and winter climbers in their own right. Having enjoyed a sporting day climbing a few gullies and exploring various parts of the mountain, they decided to glissade on their bums down a fairly steep slope, using their ice-axes to slow momentum. Big Geordie still had his crampons on and as he gathered speed, the spikes clipped the snow, causing him to somersault then hurtle uncontrollably down the mountain. He slid around 150 ft before managing to arrest the fall, but when he attempted to stand up, the pain in his ankle was excruciating and he jumped up and shot off for a further 50 ft. In complete agony, his partners tried to carry the big man without any success. They took his rucksack while Geordie used his Alpine axe as a walking stick, but he was to crash to the ground on many occasions thereafter.

The four mile return to the car park was a nightmare in the dark and by the end, he had resorted to crawling, having to negotiate streams and even hallucinating at one point. Big Geordie's friends were all ready and waiting impatiently as he made it to the car.

'Eh'l hae tae git tae A&E lads, this ankle's killin' is.'

'Well, eh could murder a pint in the Monadhliath,' said Mackie.

The big man had no choice but to join them, where he was 'forced' to sink three pints of stout before he did finally get to A&E in Dundee. The massive damage to his ligaments and a chipped bone meant that alternative pursuits such as stamp collecting and flower arranging had to be considered for a while.

Farfir from Forfar made an unplanned descent whilst on a solo winter climb over in Lochaber some years ago. Having set up camp in Glen Nevis, he'd set off for the summit of Càrn Mòr Dearg from Torlundy, taking a direct route up from the CIC Hut. Visibility had been good on the lower slopes, but the summits were now covered in a blanket of thick cloud and mist. The deep snow had turned much firmer as he made the top, prompting him to don the crampons. He decided to take a compass bearing and make for the lower summit of Càrn Dearg Mheadhonach, hoping to follow the natural ridge line back down. Conditions had become critical as the snow merged with the cloud to present a uniform sea of featureless emptiness. It was a total white-out on some very dangerous terrain.

He'd only gone 10 to 15 steps when the ground disappeared and he momentarily felt the 'whoosh' of fresh air on his body. Landing on his back, he took off like a rocket, all the while trying desperately to turn around and get his axe dug in to arrest the fall. Flailing and flapping wildly, he lunged out and managed to get the ice-pick stuck in, but nearly ripped his arm off in the process. The hand left the glove and the axe behind as Farfir continued at a horrifying pace down the mountain. As fingers were scraping frantically at the snow, he resigned himself to the thought that 'this might be the end' and waited for the final fresh air feeling before the death blow.

Mercifully, it never came and he finally slowed to a halt in a pile of old avalanche debris. For a few moments, he had no idea where he was or what he was doing, possibly suffering from a concussion, but gradually his senses returned and he took stock of his situation. The fall had taken him hundreds of feet down the Aonach Mòr side and way off route, but incredibly, he was relatively unscathed. On gathering his bearings, he had to make a dangerous and prolonged detour to get back to his tent in Glen Nevis, but this was to be a tiny sacrifice when considering what the outcome may have been.

There was a period during the 1980s and '90s when some club members felt the need to challenge themselves more in winter, having accomplished a fair level of competence on some of the more serious hillwalking routes. Johnny V Diff was at the forefront of dabbling and fancying, pushing his own boundaries. Accompanied by his long-time friend Cliffy The Jacobite, they both set off for Glen Doll in Angus and the aptly named 'Winter Corrie' on Driesh, which, when in condition, boasts an excellent choice of routes.

Their target was the 200 metre climb named Diagonal Gully. Mackie and Broonie had completed it the previous day but reported that it was in very lean condition. The signs were ominous as the night temperatures had been fairly mild and the route was now in a worse condition. A keen sense of adventure overruled common sense and with that, V Diff tied the rope on and set off up the first 30 metre pitch, which was an icy slab. He was just about at the

THE QUICK WAY DOWN

top but had been unable to place any protection. Having both crampons and axes secured into the ice, he felt comfortable and safe enough. That was until the two axes dislodged and he went for an 80 foot backflip into the void. He landed with a solid thump onto his back and was lying upside down on a 45 degree snow slope with one arm and an axe trapped underneath. He'd stopped dead but was very much alive. If he'd carried on, he would most certainly have fallen to his death. Luckily, his only ailments were feeling nauseous and a mangled arm.

It required a huge effort to get Johnny turned around and onto safer ground, where, incredibly, Cliffy suggested, 'How aboot we jist wak up to Driesh an' tak it easy?'

'How aboot eh punch you right in the pus wi' ma good ehrum?' raged V Diff. 'Git is aff this mountain ya clown!'

Back at the car, the moping Jacobite had to remove his friend's boots, then drive him to the hospital, where Johnny received a splint and the order to stay away from the mountains for a while.

For any winter walkers and climbers in Scotland, one of the biggest fears has to be getting caught in an avalanche. Jamie Mac stands alone in the club's history as being the sole member who has had the grave misfortune of enduring the full wrath of this terrifying experience, not just once, but twice.

The first incident happened while on a skiing holiday in Les Arcs in France. Along with his good lady, the pair were enjoying the scorching sunshine and idyllic Alpine setting as they casually descended, the swish of their skis gently cutting through the calm silence. But paradise was quickly about to become hell. Jamie was further ahead when he heard a faint rumble and thought some fellow skier was coming down fast behind him. When he stopped to turn and look, he realised he was about to be slammed by an avalanche which carried him over the side of the slope and tumbling down around 200 ft. Luckily, his girlfriend was able to stop just above the fault line but watched in horror as he was swept away. The piste safety crew were on the scene in a flash with their avalanche poles and dogs and able to dig him out and retrieve his skis and poles. Following a brief health assessment, he was good to go, slightly shaken but none the worse for his ordeal.

The second and more serious one occurred a couple of years later when the club were on a weekend meet at Glen Etive and staying in the fabulous Smiddy Hut at the head of the loch. The Friday night had been a lively affair with much storytelling and singing and the final 'one drink for the road' had turned into four or five more. Saturday morning was to be a later start for some, Jamie being one of them. Groups had splintered and gone to Ben Starav and Beinn Fhionnlaidh with Bruce and Mikey Fitz off sharp and heading for Stob Coir' an Albannaich. Jamie had opted to go with the latter and was way behind but able to follow their footsteps in the deep snow. He studied the old map he had and reckoned where they had gone left up a ridge; he would be able to cut across the open ground and catch them up.

The slope had steepened significantly and conditions had turned to white-out with snow falling heavily as low clouds descended. The further up he went, the angle increased and he'd resorted to driving his single axe in whilst trying to punch in with the other hand and grab onto anything he could. Then he heard the familiar rumble he'd heard a few years back, but the avalanche had passed off to his right. He thought if he headed over in that same direction, there surely wouldn't be a second avalanche. Wrong. He was now on desperately steep powdery snow, flailing about, going nowhere, when, to his horror, he heard the crack and the rumble from above. Seconds later, it crashed into him and sent him tumbling uncontrollably down the slope. Quickly, he gathered a frightening momentum sliding on his back... then nothing.

He knew he'd left the mountain for what seemed like an age and thought, 'This is the end.' He slammed down feet first into a soft bed of snow, then was engulfed moments later by the rest of the avalanche. Jamie was buried up to his neck, but luckily had one arm and shoulder free and was able to dig himself out after a huge effort. Amazingly, he'd escaped with minor bumps and pains to his limbs, but nothing serious. He did, however, have a real scare when he felt what he thought was blood running down his back and legs, but breathed a massive sigh of relief when he found it to be water from a burst drinking pouch.

In darkness, he eventually made it back down to the glen and

THE QUICK WAY DOWN

was long overdue when he reached the hut, which was in the midst of a full-blown shindig. Among the loud cheers, Big Betty bawled out, 'Ach shite, yir back. Eh wiz awa tae git fired in aboot yir kerry-oot.' The black humour and laughter masked a genuine relief that their man was home safe, as everyone had retreated during the hellish conditions that day. (Sadly and tragically, that very same day, four experienced fellow climbers were swept to their deaths in an avalanche on Bidean nam Bian in nearby Glencoe, giving a stark reminder of the seriousness and subsequent dangers of climbing the Scottish mountains in winter.)

When Big Betty received his first pair of proper winter boots from Santa, he was chomping at the bit to get out onto the hills and give them a good going over. He didn't have long to wait, as little over a week later, a sustained period of freezing temperatures in the Highlands had brought perfect conditions to the mountain playground. Joining Big Betty for the outing was his father JR, Tardy and Wee Ecky and it was a quietly excited party who headed off in the darkness of a crisp and chilly Dundee morning for the Munro pairing of Ben More and Stob Binnein near Crianlarich. The fact that this band of novice winter mountaineers made the first summit of Ben More beggared belief. Against a background of sky blue, the top half of the mountain glistened in the winter sun like a lofty skating rink. The surface was treacherous and without crampons, it was nigh on impossible.

Only Wee Ecky had the foresight to bring them while the rest tiptoed desperately upon scraps of tiny rocks protruding through the ice and cutting makeshift steps with the axes. Having safely but somewhat unsteadily descended to the bealach, JR had had enough and wisely abandoned ship via the steep west side to Benmore Glen. Rather unwisely, Tardy and Big Betty pressed on, slipping and sliding behind Wee Ecky, who made short work of the steep, icy north ridge of Stob Binnein. It was now mid-afternoon and the temperature was plummeting as the sun dropped lower. After labouring wearily for some 200 ft, the pairing of Tardy and Big Betty grudgingly threw in the towel and admitted defeat. Their bodies chilled quickly as they waited for Wee Ecky's return from the summit, so in the meantime, Big Betty had the bright idea of attempting an ice-break with his axe.

In layman's terms, this meant deliberately sliding down a controlled slope which would have a clear and smooth run out, then leaning the body weight on the axe to arrest or halt the slide. In theory, this should work like a dream. In practice… well. Big Betty chose a near vertical wall of 20 ft, which was dangerously close to the huge drop of the eastern corrie. He'd also failed to notice the large boulder field situated way below. Facing into the wall, he edged his way along, kicking into the solid snow, then shouted to Tardy, 'Here, these new boots are magic, grippin' brilliant.' Two seconds later, 'whoosh' and off he went. Wearing a full set of waterproofs is not the ideal clothing when one is looking for some friction on ice. Tardy later commented that if he'd been in the luge event, Big Betty could easily have won a Winter Olympic gold medal, such was the speed he accelerated at. The ice-axe, which was meant to halt the slide, was bouncing around wildly as a distant spectator attached to his wrist.

At maximum speed, the big man shot through two huge boulders headfirst. Two feet on either side and his head would have smashed right through his arse. It was then he hit the boulder field and came to an abrupt halt. A guardian angel pleasantly called down, 'it's not your time,' which reassured Betty no end. He lay there for a moment and couldn't believe he was still alive. Then he felt his left thigh, which seemed like twice the width it usually was. 'That's nuhin,' he thought. 'Ehm stull alehv,' and smiled. He glanced back up the hill and saw Tardy, his brother-in-arms, his comrade, his right-hand man, literally crying, laughing at this tragic misfortune. Where they come from, as long as no one dies, then it's fair game to indulge in howls of laughter and piss-taking for being so stupid.

'Are ya arite?' he eventually got out through tears of laughter.

'Well apert fae a leg that feels like itz been run ower fae a steam-roller, eh feel brand new,' he winced.

Wee Ecky soon appeared with two English climbers who saw the distress Big Betty was in and without a second thought, they each took an under arm so that the injured man could at least hobble down, albeit in extreme agony. Due to the steepness and risky condition of the slope, the usual route to Benmore Glen was a no-no. The only alternative was to climb down the east side and what would prove to be a horrendous descent in the dark, following the Allt Coire Chaorach river, at times actually in the river to avoid the dense forestry. It was four hours of hell before they made it to the A85 road and some distance from their start point at Benmore Farm. With a huge stroke of luck, the headlights from a car came into view and out popped JR, who had been frantically driving back and forth searching for the group. The two English lads were thanked for their incredible act of selflessness and kindness and taken back to their car, then the quartet pulled into the nearby Luib Hotel. Big Betty phoned his wife to tell her what had happened and she instantly burst into tears.

'Dinna worry,' he reassured his good lady, 'wir in the boozer haein a few pints then ehl head inta A&E on the weh hame.' This calmed her down considerably, knowing her man was in the safe environs of a warm hostelry, scooping flagons of ale after nearly dying. (The poor woman's reply was mostly unprintable. He did, however, make it to A&E with a belly full of stout, where an examination confirmed no cracked bones, just advice to rest and the purchase of a pair of crampons.)

Final Munro summit parties are always eagerly anticipated within the club and a full contingent of weekenders boarded the minibus to join Wee Ecky and celebrate on Am Bàisteir on the Isle of Skye. Shenanigans, merriment and sing-songs ensued as they made the long journey north and west one Friday night and it was a rather groggy and bedraggled mob who assembled outside the tents on a glorious sunny morning. Hangovers were soon forgotten as the party, led by the kilted Wee Ecky, took the route over Bruach na Frithe before descending into the spectacular Coire a' Bhàsteir under the intimidating north face of Am Bàisteir. It was here that Dougie Mac unexpectedly said goodbye to the rest and began climbing the near-vertical face.

Cries of 'Dougie, dinna go up there, yull git yirsel killed man,' fell on deaf ears as he took off like a mountain goat. He nearly wiped out the whole group when, around 50 ft up he dislodged a massive boulder, which saw men scatter in all directions as it exploded right on the spot where moments earlier they had gathered. Another couple came crashing down in rapid succession as they quickly departed for the east ridge. Having negotiated the bad step safely, they continued up the beautifully exposed ridge to perch on top of the airy summit. Wee Ecky was congratulated by all as Big Betty fired into 'Bonnie Dundee' on the pipes. When he finished, loud cheers rang out from fellow climbers on the neighbouring peaks of Sgùrr nan Gillean and Bruach na Frithe. The champagne was popped and the malt whisky passed around as cries went over the north face, 'Dougie, wahr are ya?'

The men reckoned he should have been up and joining them by now. It was at this moment that two members of the party came up to share the horrific news that someone had seen Dougie falling. Knowing the severity of the face, everyone expected the worst and was certain their friend would be dead. It was with massive relief when Cammy managed to get along to him and relay that he was alive but in a very bad way. Dougie said sheepishly, 'I've been a very silly boy.'

He remembered being near to the top but had no recollection of the fall, possibly due to smashing his head. Although he had multiple fractures all over his body, having fallen some 200 ft, there were four huge contributing factors which meant he survived. The first being he'd landed on a sloping narrow ledge, which, if he'd gone over that, it was another sheer drop of 60 ft, which would most certainly have finished him. The next was a fellow climber who was also a doctor and tended to him on the spot. Another climber had one of the early mobile phones and was able to call the Mountain Rescue. The helicopter pilot did an outstanding job hovering with his blades very near to the cliff face in order to drop his winchman down and collect Dougie. He was taken to Glasgow's Southern General hospital, where he spent some time recuperating and, although he suffered from a fair amount of memory loss, he went on to make a full recovery. However, his mad days of the 'Dougie Mac tours' were over.

(In all but two of the aforementioned incidents and falls, each climber found it necessary and indeed their duty to get themselves off the mountain and down to safety, so long as they were able to, often in severe pain and miles from their start point. There was never a second thought given to calling out the Mountain Rescue when those guys could be needed for much more serious incidents. There also wasn't the access to mobile phones, which admittedly, have proven invaluable in proper rescues and sadly, recoveries. However, in this modern era of huge numbers taking to the mountains and phones never out of hand, it is all too easy to 'make the call' for instances which the old school would view as downright trivial. Read Doug Scott and Chris Bonnington's epic account of descending The Ogre in the Karakoram, severely injured or Joe Simpson's monumental retreat (also, severely injured) from Siula Grande in Peru if any inspiration is needed on self-rescue.)

CHAPTER 16

The Bothy Culture

Culra bothy

THE WORD BOTHY, as we know it today, more than likely derives from the Scottish Gaelic word *bothan* (pronounced bo'-han), meaning hut, booth or shelter and also an illegal drinking den for men in days gone by. A great many of the modern-day bothies have risen from the remnants of homes abandoned by long-gone generations and been brought back to life from that of their former deserted and decaying shells of four lonely stone walls by the dedicated voluntary work of the magnificent MBA – Mountain Bothy Association. (Interested readers can find a detailed and extensive history on their website.) Of course, not all bothies are linked to the MBA and a good few exist independently on various estates.

These often hard to get to and at times, very remote dwellings have been sought out and used extensively during the club's history. A great many like-minded outdoor enthusiasts have done likewise in search of peace, solitude, camaraderie, far-flung mountain summits, deerstalking and fish-laden rivers and lochs.

Years ago, the bothy experience seemed to be more of an underground activity with a bigger sense of adventure and anticipation as to what lay ahead when searching for them. Much effort was put into studying where these tiny squares were located on an OS map and what obstacles or river crossings had to be negotiated. Back then, information was generally passed on by word of mouth, whereas nowadays, the internet (and the odd book) provides pictures, videos, grid references and highly detailed directions on how to reach them.

The preparation for a bothy trip begins with the rucksack and what to take. It is of paramount importance to pack all the essentials such as clothing, food, cooker, map, compass, torch, sleeping bag and a mat as each person must be self-sufficient in the wilderness. The weight of the pack, however, rises considerably when one includes the 'real' essentials of a large carry-out. There have been bothy meets when grown men have almost been reduced to tears due to alcohol stocks running dry during the fireside ceilidh. When coal, logs and kindling for the fire are added, the pack becomes a very heavy burden indeed. Many of the male members have taken great pride in the macho competition of carrying the heaviest loads, where any individuals caught in possession of lesser loads were verbally demolished.

Some of the bothy poems included within these pages have documented the foolhardy practice of indulging in a bevvy session before the serious undertaking of a long march, usually in the dark. What seemed like a great laugh soon turns to hell when the small caravan (on a few occasions with a 10kg bag of coal) is heaved onto the back and any incline on the track resembles the slopes of Everest. Some have tumbled and fallen, some have gone headfirst into freezing rivers, some have blatantly 'misplaced' their coal or wood, some have missed the bothy completely and wandered around aimlessly in the dark and others have just curled up in the heather and wished they were at home in a cosy bed. It is fair to say that battling through pathless terrain in wild weather, half-canned and lost, has to be the most soul-destroying scenario of them all, especially in the middle of a torrential downpour and the waterproofs and head torch have been recklessly placed at the bottom of the pack. But then again, it certainly builds character. Some of the big walks, such as Barrisdale, Ben Alder Cottage, Maol Bhuidhe and Sourlies, are enough to test even the fittest when fully laden.

Many years ago, a contingent from the club was heading to the small estate bothy near the foot of Meall Chuaich and were, as usual, a little worse for wear, some more than others, it has to be said. In the dark, they staggered east following the track parallel to the aqueduct, which transfers water from Loch Cuaich down to Loch Eireachd. Someone, who was part of the 'worse for wear' group, managed to stumble away from the track and straight into the fast-flowing water, which swept them off downstream. Thankfully, their ride on Scotland's largest flume came to an abrupt halt at a grid covering a pipe entrance and they were gratefully hauled out by some friends who thought this was hilarious.

The bothy of 'Blackburn of Pattack' has long since gone to the great bothy graveyard in the sky, but back in its heyday of smoke-filled, lung-choking residence, it was a wee hoose popular with the club. On a wild night of heavy snowfall, the minibus had pulled into a hostelry in Dalwhinnie to appease the drunken human cargo and allow them some further refreshments. As the drams and ale began flowing in earnest, a local man politely enquired as to where the men were going on such a foul night.

'Ach, wir on oor weh tae the bothy at Loch Pattack,' came the answer.

'I wouldn't be taking the bus over the moor,' said the concerned man. 'The drifts are horrendous.'

'Ach dinna worry, pal. We're fae Dundee an' a wee but o' sna winna stop us,' came the slurred reply.

When at length it was time to leave, the local man watched with a look of 'well, I warned you' as the bus lights disappeared into the blizzard.

As they trundled and skidded along by Loch Eireachd, Big Geordie piped up, 'Horrendous sna drifts ma erse. That boy wiz bletherin' shite!'

And as predictable as 'drunk men know best,' they hit a huge snow drift just as they were accelerating uphill. A ramshackle work party set about digging the bus out with ice axes flailing dangerously close to fellow navvies. Amazingly, they managed to free the vehicle and turn it on a sixpence, thus allowing the older members to beat a hasty retreat, where they spent a very uncomfortable and freezing night on the bus back near Dalwhinnie. The young bucks opted for the dismal march through appallingly deep snow, shouldering heavy packs and carrying bags of precious liquid gold and ale. It was the wee small hours before the exhausted men crawled into the bothy. The old brigade did eventually join their comrades the following day for the fireside fling and were rewarded with a room full of smoke as thick as that of the Victorian smog of London.

The wonderful and truly calamitous list of mishaps whilst attempting to locate and get into bothies could easily fill a few chapters on their own, but there can be no finer moment than when that familiar smell of smoke from a fire signals the bothy is near. A flickering candle in a window and the sound of hearty laughter and song from a gathered congregation, each wearing a warm glow from the dancing inferno, is as close to bothy Shangri-La as it gets. Although there was one memorable occasion when this vision of paradise was actually trumped in spectacular fashion.

A group of seven men were heading to Invermallie bothy late one night, following the track by the shores of Loch Arkaig, when, on approach, the sound of music could be heard from within.

'Ach somebody must hae a signal on thir radio.'

'Dinna be daft, ya canna git a signal oot here.'

As the door creaked open, an almost Brigadoon-like scene was playing out around a roaring fire. A large group of musicians from Edinburgh had arrived earlier and were now involved in a full-on shindig. An uilleann piper was sitting in the corner, his fingers rattling the chanter as he hammered out a set of jigs and reels, most ably accompanied by a pair of guitarists who were strumming like lunatics. Two fiddlers and a penny whistler were also involved in trading beautifully woven harmonies in the musical melee as another character kept time, thrashing his bodhran with expert rhythmic beats while his right boot crashed on the wooden floor.

Johnny V Diff was almost in tears as he cried out, 'Eh think wiv jist died an' walked through the gates o' Bothy Heaven.'

The rest agreed and wasted no time in laying out their sleeping bags upstairs, then squeezed in to all available space in the crowded room. Carry-outs, which were carefully rationed for two nights, didn't stand a chance and were wholly demolished, such was the power of this ceilidh to top all ceilidhs, which duly danced deep into the wee small hours. The musicians couldn't believe that the Dundee contingent would be up in a few hours' time and nursing thumping hangovers while walking all the way out to the Munro pairing of Meall na Teanga and Sròn a' Choire Ghairbh and back in a monsoon. The Saturday edition of the Invermallie horo gheallaidh was already in full swing when the mountain men returned, but for them it was a very knackered, subdued and sober affair compared to that of the previous night. For those lucky enough to have been there, it will always remain the greatest bothy weekend ever.

A huge part of the bothy culture is, of course, the unique and varied characters one often meets when stepping through their doors. People come from all walks of life and different social backgrounds with many contrasting and diverse outlooks and views thrown into the pot of comment, storytelling and debate. There can be no better evenings around a roaring fire than those spent with like-minded individuals or groups sharing a passion for the great outdoors, a few drams, the craic and riotous sing-songs.

There are those, however, who are looking for a completely alternative experience, possibly craving the peace, tranquillity and solitude of these remote dwellings. True, not everyone is there to indulge in a fireside ceilidh and it isn't the first time and certainly won't be the last, when some angry voice has called from a sleeping bag next door to 'KEEP THE BLOODY NOISE DOWN!' Admittedly, arriving at midnight or later in a group then putting flame to the hearth while cracking open the malt, isn't everyone's idea of a great night, especially when the shindig crawls deep into the wee small hours. The tables are usually turned though, when the offended individuals rise at the crack of dawn to stomp around loudly while clanging pots and pans, much to the misery of the heavily hungover revellers.

THE BOTHY CULTURE

One bitterly cold February night, ten members had arrived late at Gorton bothy to find someone curled snugly in their bag. As the fire burst into life and the whisky was uncorked, the character rose from his slumber and joined the gathering. It turned out to be Norrie Muir, one of the old climbers from the legendary Creagh Dhu Mountaineering Club, who regaled the company with past stories of that most rugged but hugely talented climbing band of working-class men.

The memorable nights of drunken camaraderie spent with complete strangers are aplenty, but there has also been a fair share of characters considered to be borderline 'crackpots' or just 'different' from the rough and tumble of the NCR.

The weather was wild and unforgiving as the group descended from the summit of Càrn Dearg and it wasn't long before some of the others welcomed their return to Culra bothy with a blazing fire and a room full of laughter and warmth. As Fred quietly sipped on his dram, he casually said, 'Wiv got a right belter through in oor room. The guy is sittin' in absolutely soakin' gear, starin' at the wall wi' a wee candle fir company. Eh telt him to come through an' git a heat at the fire, but he never sade a word.'

'Mibbee he's an escaped axe-murderer jist waitin' fir ah o' us to go to sleep the' night,' laughed Geordie. The rest laughed along nervously with the big man, but secretly worried that it might be true as imaginations ran riot following the throw-away comment. By early morning, though, the loner was gone and the men were grateful their heads (although thumping) were still attached to their shoulders.

Big Betty and Joe had cursed almost every step they had taken since leaving Bob Scott's on their way to Corrour. The Lairig Ghru track had transformed into a lethal skating rink and with both men heavily laden with a cargo of wood, coal and whisky (and other less important necessities, none of which included crampons), it was an uneven battle to stay upright and many times they crashed on the icy surface. Following a stiff and hard climb to the tip of Bod an Deamhain, the weary pair returned to the bothy and readied themselves for a night of alcoholic mirth and merriment. (This Munro does, of course, translate to 'Penis of the Demon', which these days is more commonly known as The Devil's Point and does indeed suggest that the Gaels had a great sense of humour. Nowhere is this more evident than at nearby Royal Deeside, where Cac Càrn Mòr (Big Shite Hill) and Cac Càrn Beag (Little Shite Hill) stand proud and commanding overlooking a royal playground. Hilarious it was to see the pair somewhat hastily and conveniently renamed 'Lochnagar' as the mere mention of the word 'cac' in these parts would surely cause great unease and distress to those who have never heard sweary words before).

Joe and Big Betty's inferno did very little to heat the spartan old bothy, especially with a howling icy gale blasting under the large gap in the door, but the whisky was doing a sterling job at warming the soul. The men were joined by a pair of English climbers who were fairly reluctant to engage in any real conversation and almost immediately slid into their sleeping bags to cook some food. Shortly afterwards, they were bedded down for the night. Their chance of any sleep, however, for the next seven hours, was slim to absolutely zero.

The drams got larger, the laughter and singing got louder, the banter got wilder and the air, for the most part, was an industrial blue, straight from the factory floor in Dundee.

'Here lads, are yiz waantin' a wee dram?'

'Eh, mon jine the perty. Gaun gie wiz a wee English folk sang, mon.'

The NCR lads were relentless in their efforts to get the climbers out of their bags and involved in the fireside soiree. After declining many offers, one of them finally said, 'We've had a long day climbing and just want to sleep. We don't drink but do play in our local church band.'

'Aww fir fuck sake,' slurred Joe. 'Sorry aboot the fuckin' swearin'. Wih didna ken ya wir Bible-thumpers. Wull treh an' keep the noise doon an' lit yiz git back to sleep.'

If truth be told, there was more chance of them getting beamed up to the Starship Enterprise than getting a kip and the situation was exasperated further when two of Joe's mates clattered into the bothy around 2.00am and set about reigniting the fire and carrying on the party till 5.00am. The poor English lads must have been like a pair of zombies walking out to their car at Linn o' Dee that morning.

When bodies are already in a bothy, there is nothing better than to be greeted with a friendly and hearty welcome. This wasn't the case, however, when four club members made the long and challenging trek into the remote bothy of Bearnais way over on the west coast. Imagine their surprise when they found the door locked from the inside and a man and two women sat by the fire trying to ignore the knocks on the window and calls to open the door. They'd obviously planned on having it for themselves and it was a bit of a Mexican stand-off before the male occupant very reluctantly opened the door. As one can imagine, the mood was toxic with no pleasantries exchanged and the weekend felt more like a month spent in a library.

When many of the usual weekend regulars had called off with a whole host of lame excuses, Cammy and Big Betty had decided to honour the proposed date and attend the meet to Over Phawhope bothy in the Borders. The pair viewed their serene surroundings while watching the sun go down and partying like this day would be their last on the planet. Extreme contentment accompanied both pished men as they wriggled into their sleeping bags and bid each other a peaceful goodnight.

Five hours later, Cammy's eyes cracked open to a room full of daylight and the reek of stale whisky and ale. He glanced out of the window and nearly shat his bag as there, not 20 ft away, positioned on a picnic table in the garden was an Elmer Fudd-type character in full camouflage gear, surveying the landscape through the scope of a high velocity rifle. Thankfully, they were pleasant enough and not looking to bag any big game hillwalkers on this particular occasion, but once they'd moved on, the men agreed that the posturing and machismo act of boys with their big toys was done to impress.

'Ehm too bliddee hungower to be impressed wi' that shite,' said Betty.

'Eh same here mate,' added Cammy. 'Eh feel like the boy shot is in the nut through the night though. Mon, let's get the brekkies on an' git these hills done.'

During one of the annual camping weekends to Glenfinnan, two of the crew had opted to walk into Corryhully bothy but not before getting tanked up in a local bar. The hour was very late when Bruce and Davie San donned their heavy packs and staggered along the track heading for the railway viaduct. Although they were half-canned the pace was brisk as they marched in with head torches switched off to preserve battery life.

All of a sudden, Bruce hit the deck hard and was crying out in agony. Davie who was just a few steps behind asked, 'Wut the hell are ya daein doon there?'

'Ehv jist been skelped in the pus wi' an anvil,' wailed Bruce.

As torchlights were switched back on the culprit was revealed in the form of a large steel gate which had taken out Bruce's top front teeth. Both men clambered around the ground looking for the broken ivories before Davie stopped, still crying with laughter and said, 'If we do find them, are we jist stickin' them back in wi' chewin' gum?'

The pain from the cold air hitting the nerves was excruciating. When they finally reached the bothy Doctor Davie's remedy was to fill a bottle cap with whisky then told his pal to keep the stumps bathing in it. Predictably, this helped not a jot and Bruce spent the whole weekend curled up on the bus in horrendous agony while his comrades bagged mountains and got soundly blootered. For many bothy regulars, there truly is no finer feeling than when the fire is crackling, the drams are flowing and a group of strangers are sharing stories and laughter in complete harmony with one another. However, on those very, very rare occasions, sometimes a wolf in sheep's clothing mingles with the flock to bring utter chaos to a beautiful gathering. The club had taken a big group to a bothy way up in the north west Highlands and had spent the Friday night revelling into the wee small hours. Three strangers had appeared on the Saturday afternoon while the men were out on the hills and had taken over the main room where the fire was, laying all their bedding out on the floor and obviously staking a claim to ownership of the room.

As any civil bothy-goer will agree, the main room is the party room and sleeping arrangements are usually taken in other rooms when available, which they were. The NCR lads returned to find an awkward situation but kindly informed the new arrivals that they would have to move their sleeping bags until it was candles out time later… which would be VERY later. The night was pleasant enough with stories shared and songs being sung, but the new arrivals had clocked out early, having demolished their carry-outs and were now soundly sleeping where they sat. Or so the rest thought. Big Geordie had noticed that the 'wolf' had stirred and had very stealthily tucked a knife up the inside of his wrist to conceal it. When questioned on his cowardly actions, he addressed the company by saying, 'You Dundee bastards better get tae yir beds,' hoping to intimidate and, in doing so, clear the room so the trio could get their beds laid out. The joyful and peaceful mood turned instantly into one of shock and anger. Big Betty thought about his young son and father who were now sleeping, but earlier, had been innocently sitting near to the blade man. An overwhelming rage exploded inside him and retribution was delivered to the wolf in the form of a huge right-hander, quickly followed by a left, then right again. In the middle of nowhere, the law of the street was administered without a second thought.

At times, the in-house humour has been cutting and brutal, with a healthy helping of stupidity thrown in, which those on the outside would look upon as childish and reckless. The men, however, thought it was hilarious when someone had crashed out due to some over-indulgence on the bevvy and sought to balance items such as boots, cans of beer, pots and pans and anything else that came to hand, on their heads. One drunk member's toes were once used to hold a lit candle for a while and slipping a chocolate bar into the crack of an inebriated, sleeping man's arse brought many tears of laughter to the perpetrators.

Placing various items into fellow members' sleeping bags was not uncommon but when the bold Sir Lancelot received a large cast-iron horse's head in his bag (in a scene mimicking *The Godfather* film), he took umbrage and threw it out where it almost crashed through the upstairs floorboards. Falling asleep during a fireside ceilidh was always seen as a most punishable crime and this would take the form of tying the guilty man's boot or shoe laces together in a hundred knots. In the wee sma oors when the candles had burned out and the fire had died, the results were spectacular as the guilty man could be heard crashing through tables and chairs in total darkness. For those who remember the near-vertical old staircase in Shenavall bothy, Russell 'The Cyclist' fell down it not once, but two nights in a row. Copious amounts of red wine may have been involved, causing most of his body to turn black and blue and giving him an incredibly long and painful walk out, which the others thought was hysterical.

The rules of engagement for black humour were simple – no quarter given and none ever received.

These then are just a small selection of the numerous stories, incidents and characters from the NCR's very own back catalogue of life in the bothy culture and who knows, maybe some day our paths will cross with a few of you in some far-flung dwelling, hopefully with a roaring fire and healthy drams passing lips to toast these wonderful places.

Epilogue

IN DECEMBER 2024, the club celebrated its 75th anniversary during the annual Xmas Meet and how very apt it was to be held in the fabulous Càrn Dearg Mountaineering Club Hut in Glen Clova, a club with which the NCR had many dual members in the early days and a glen which sits warmly in the hearts of everyone from the past to the present day.

In 1949, no one could have imagined the monumental changes that would take place throughout the coming years and how utterly different daily life is in this world we know today. The outdated clothing, footwear, tents and gear have advanced to unprecedented levels of quality, comfort and reliability and will no doubt keep improving in the future.

The popularity of hillwalking, mountaineering, Munro-bagging and camping has exploded in recent years, possibly due to the internet and the mass sharing of photos, videos and routes on social media. There are those who will argue for it and those who will argue against it, but the fact of the matter is, the game has changed forever and it is not just confined to the British Isles. One only has to look at the depressing images of massive queues snaking up and down Mount Everest, which now sadly, has the highest 'unofficial' graveyard and rubbish tip in the world. At home, it is not uncommon on many weekends to see trails of human ants trudging wearily up the more popular mountains such as Nevis, Lawers and Ben Lomond. The thought of following a multitude of boots and arses of all shapes and sizes to the summit becomes very unappealing. Chuck in the occasional items of discarded rubbish, human waste and the reek of marijuana and the Great Outdoors doesn't seem so great any more.

Some bothies too have had to accommodate huge numbers and although this isn't something new, it can happen and arguably, with a clientele which these great wee shelters were not intended for. During a recent visit to Ruigh Aiteachain, the bothy felt more like an Airbnb with families on holiday and bairns running riot. There was a similar situation in the excellent Lookout on Skye, with families using it for a holiday.

The club revisited Glendhu bothy some years ago and when visiting numbers swelled to 24, it felt very cramped and cosy indeed. On many occasions, it has been the NCR who have done the donkey work and carried large amounts of fuel in so that everyone can enjoy the main attraction, which is the fire. Whilst talking to a pair of French mountain bikers, the question was asked how they found out about such a remote dwelling. Their answer came as a bit of a shock when they replied, 'We found it in a local magazine advertising 'free accommodation' in Scotland.' When they asked where the nearest shop was to pick up food supplies, they were politely told it would be 'a bit of a pedal'. Completely unprepared, their faces dropped.

Admittedly, it would be very naive to say that the NCR didn't take a dozen or so bodies to a bothy in days gone by, but they were, of course, different times and never once was the place overcrowded, as they mostly had it to themselves. And yes, two coachloads rough-camping in Kintail would be viewed as excessive numbers converging on one area. Back in the day, many publicans were much more accommodating with wild camping nearby and mostly encouraged to bring in some very healthy revenue. These practices would be totally unmanageable nowadays due to the sheer volume of people camping and those in camper vans.

As the NCR club looks forward now, hoping there will be a member who will write the next chapter in 75 years, it is only right to end this story and say what an absolute honour and privilege it has been to walk each and every step of those hard miles across this beautiful land we call Scotland in the company of great friends. The kind of friends who would covertly plant a large rock in your rucksack, then howl with laughter when you found it much later, after carrying it for miles. Or the devious and cunning ones who would wait until you got halfway over a river crossing, then totally soak you with a bombardment of huge stones. Or the plain crazy ones who would fire a volley of snowballs at you when you needed to concentrate while climbing and stay attached to the mountain. And of course, who could forget those who took great delight back in the day of stealthily grabbing your camera from your pack and secretly taking a photo of you having a private dump on the hillside, then cry with laughter a week later when your photos got developed and you relayed how you proudly showed your family the 'not-so-beautiful' scenery. All for one and one for all.

The 'Wild Mountain Times' were indeed wild and mostly hilarious, but the final words of thanks are reserved for the unsung heroes of the Mountain Rescue, the volunteers who maintain the mountain tracks, the people of the Mountain Bothy Association and last but not least, the publicans who made sure the NCR throats never run dry. Slainte.

Luath Press Limited

committed to publishing well written books worth reading

LUATH PRESS takes its name from Robert Burns, whose little collie Luath (*Gael.*, swift or nimble) tripped up Jean Armour at a wedding and gave him the chance to speak to the woman who was to be his wife and the abiding love of his life. Burns called one of the 'Twa Dogs' Luath after Cuchullin's hunting dog in Ossian's *Fingal*. Luath Press was established in 1981 in the heart of Burns country, and is now based a few steps up the road from Burns' first lodgings on Edinburgh's Royal Mile. Luath offers you distinctive writing with a hint of unexpected pleasures.

Most bookshops in the UK, the US, Canada, Australia, New Zealand and parts of Europe, either carry our books in stock or can order them for you. To order direct from us, please send a £sterling cheque, postal order, international money order or your credit card details (number, address of cardholder and expiry date) to us at the address below. Please add post and packing as follows: UK – £1.00 per delivery address; overseas surface mail – £2.50 per delivery address; overseas airmail – £3.50 for the first book to each delivery address, plus £1.00 for each additional book by airmail to the same address. If your order is a gift, we will happily enclose your card or message at no extra charge.

Luath Press Limited
543/2 Castlehill
The Royal Mile
Edinburgh EH1 2ND
Scotland
Telephone: 0131 225 4326 (24 hours)
Email: sales@luath.co.uk
Website: www.luath.co.uk